Failsworth Born

Ben Brierley was born on Sunday 26th June 1825 in Failsworth, Lancashire. For those who have never heard of the place, it can be just about seen on a map, trapped in between Manchester and Oldham. It had its own Urban District Council until 1974, when boundary changes plunged it into Oldham in the County of Greater Manchester. Ben *would* have been pleased!

Ben's father, James, was a native of Middleton and earned his living as a hand-loom weaver. He had served as a soldier in the Napoleonic Wars and is said to have fought at Antwerp and Leipzig under General Strangeways, but at the time of his discharge was a gunner in Major E C Whinyates' Rocket Troop, part of the Rocket Brigade of the Royal Horse Artillery. This was present at Waterloo and was sent to England to be reduced at the end of 1815. James's turn to go came in July 1816, when his discharge certificate showed that he had enlisted at the age of seventeen and had served "From 2nd April 1812, to July, 1816, 4 years, 119 days." His service at Waterloo counted for an extra two years, so the total assessed was "6 years, 119 days". He had signed a receipt to say that he had received "all just Demands of Pay, Clothing, etc" due to him and at the age of twenty-one was 5'7" tall with light hair, grey eyes and a fresh complexion. James was also present at "Peterloo" in 1819 - perhaps one of Sam Bamford's contingent of Middleton weavers, though he must have married about this time and settled in Failsworth.

Ben's mother Esther (née Whitehead), otherwise known as "Jacky wife", sang in the choir of All Saints, Newton Heath, under the baton of James Ridings, father of Elijah (of whom more later). Ben was baptised in this church by the Reverend Thomas Gaskell when he was not quite two months old, and one of his earliest memories was of hearing his mother sing. "Her voice was a powerful contralto; and I can remember its clear mellow tones so far in the past as I can remember anything. I can hear them now." She had four children, two boys and two girls, before Ben arrived. The baptisms of Anne (4th November 1821) and of Nancy (14th September 1823) are recorded in the registers of All Saints, Newton Heath but there is no trace of the boys. All four children died in infancy, before Ben was born. Such were the times, and Esther Brierley herself did not see old age. She died of stomach cancer in their canalside home at Hollinwood in the autumn of 1854. Ben wrote of his mother at this later period of her life, "She was a gentle creature; and like the [illegible] in 'Macbeth' [illegible] lived.' N[illegible] acquaintanc[illegible] more than she, or bore her sufferings with truer fortitude... It was her deep religious feeling that was her support in all her travails, and gave her cheerfulness when physical pain had her in its grip."

Prima Pizza and the Bridge Inn in 1995. The plaque commemorating Ben's birth can be seen beneath the first floor window in the centre of the photograph

Before Ben was four years old he had a brother: "I did not give him the heartiest welcome, as I had fears that he might claim a joint possession of my spoon. I hated the sight of 'Owd Jacky Wife' for bringing him into the world, and had serious thoughts of damaging her 'parsley bed' by the introduction of cats. But 'Little Tummy' grew into my liking as he grew more plump, and I allowed him to suck most of my farthing 'humbug'." Tommy grew up to become an Oldham policeman. He soon gained promotion and rose swiftly through the ranks, but was struck down by fever and is buried in Chadderton. His eldest daughter, Nancy Brierley, signed his death certificate with an X - at the age of seventeen, she was illiterate, yet Thomas and Ben weren't.

Part of the dwelling in which our hero was born still stands, forming the foundation of number 466 Oldham Road. It is, at the time of writing, the Prima Pizza Parlour. Before that it was an Indian takeaway and before that, amongst other things, it was "Uncle Jack's Toffee Shop". I remember it well. Masonic expert Clare Dunkerley tells me that in the 1970s the building was occupied by the late Ronald Badley, once the Master of the Ben Brierley Masonic Lodge, which was consecrated in 1908. Ben, a Mason himself, might well have commented, "Whey, mon, that caps o'!"

This is an illustrious stretch of road. Clare Dunkerley, himself Worshipful Master of the Ben Brierley Lodge in 1958 and a member for over fifty years, was born at 64 Old Road. If you were to stand in front of Ben's birthplace and count to five hundred as you made your way to Clare's scene of nativity, before you reached two hundred you would be passing the birthplace of Elijah Ridings, who encouraged Ben so much in his early years. Carry on counting, and at four hundred and fifty 64a would be passed - the birthplace of Joseph Burgess, youthful poet, journalist and campaigner for the Independent Labour Party; his autobiography, "A Potential Poet?", makes fascinating reading. What a brainy lot from such a small area! It could be summed up by the motto in plain English under the Failsworth coat of arms: "True worth never fails". Except for the house where Elijah saw the light of day, the buildings still stand.

Today, a plaque set in the brickwork marks Ben's birthplace - though not the bedroom where he was born, as many people think. A word or two from Ben hissel' will explain why: "The upper portion of the house has since been rebuilt; and now forms a dwelling of itself, the lower part, in which I groped my way when I began to toddle and go into mischief, now serving only as a foundation. In the original plan of the building there was a door communicating with the principal bed-room and the road. This door served more purposes than one. Besides affording a means of escape when the basement was flooded, as was often the case, it was a convenience for drunken people to use their clogs against. Many a time have I listened to the music thus produced when wakened out of my childish dreams, as these serenades were more frequent than agreeable. The only peace we had was when my grandfather, who lived within a few doors, was constable."

The place was called The Rocks, but, "Do not imagine," says Ben, "that my earliest home was among the mountains... The humble tenement in which I first saw what should have been light, is situated in a hole caused by the raising of the road, so as to be on a level with the bridge that spans the Rochdale canal at Failsworth." Part of the downward-sloping wedge-shaped area is still in existence and was called The Rocks because it was walled with stone. Ben "was placed at the thin end", where the houses were flooded to a depth of several feet by a great thunderstorm of 1831. But the Brierleys had gone by then; Ben only lived in Failsworth for the first five years of his life. I wonder if his removal had anything to do with what happened to him at Failsworth Pole.

William IV succeeded to the throne in 1830 and to honour the event the (first) Failsworth Pole was taken down, regilded and repainted, and returned to its original lofty position. An ox was walked round the lanes of Failsworth, then slaughtered and part of it roasted in front of the Crown and Cushion; a stew was made from the remainder of the beast and served out to whoever came along. Ben's mother sent him with a jug to collect some of the meat juices and what happened next made quite an impression on the five-year-old boy. When he presented himself, the woman doling it out pushed him aside. "Nawe, thou mun ha' noane," she said; "thy gronfeyther's a Jacobin." (The term "Jacobin" originally meant a member of a French political club, but by this time was used as an expression of contempt for any political reformer. It should not be confused with "Jacobite", which means an adherent of James II after he fled to France in 1688. Quite a difference!) Ben went away with an empty jug and without understanding the remark, "but those words have rung in my ears ever since. They set me a-thinking, and I wondered what sort of an animal a Jacobin was that his little starving grandson could have no soup. This treatment had much to do with the formation of my political character, and as I grew up I felt determined I would never belong to a party which made me suffer for what my grandfather believed."

If I'd been Ben Brierley, I would have had nothing more to do with Failsworth poles, but Ben was made of sterner stuff. Nearly sixty years later he was the principal speaker at the inauguration of the (third) pole in 1889.

Perhaps he was grateful for his early education at "Th'owd Skoo" on Pole Lane. A large needlework canvas depicting Failsworth Old School hangs in the Public Library, informing the observer that it was erected by public subscription in the year 1785 and that Mr Birch was the founder.

Tis built on a rock though tempest may rave,
Its solid foundation repels the proud wave.

It was done as a present for Victoria and Esther Clough and bears the legend "Jane Clough's work July 31st 1855."

Ben was to return here, too, in more boisterous times, but more of that

The Rocks, photographed in the 1880s. The thin end of the wedge had already been filled in and the houses in the distance rebuilt from first floor level

later. For the present, suffice it to say that he remembered the school as a place where all denominations were welcome and where he had the pleasure of winning three marbles for spelling "victuals" correctly.

The Move to Hollinwood

The Brierleys couldn't escape water, for they settled in Canal Street, Hollinwood, on the very towpath of the Manchester and Ashton Canal. The site is now covered by the Roxy cinema's car park, but with the M66 due to come through shortly, goodness knows what it will be in a year or two.

The cottage had not been vacated when the family arrived with their "sticks"; the woman of the house was busy baking and a lame boy was operating the loom. Another lame boy, Fred Kearsley, hobbled nearby and Ben wondered if he had been brought into a society of cripples. I'm sure that Fred was the inspiration for the character of Humpy Dick, who appears in "Cast Upon the World", a partly autobiographical work covering the years Ben spent in Hollinwood. Ben claimed that this character caused more difficulty and sorrow to write about than all the rest of his characters put together.

The move to Hollinwood saw the end of Ben's full-time schooling, as he was needed to wind bobbins for his father, who worked on the loom. His days at "Th'owd Skoo" on Pole Lane, Failsworth, were *over* at an age when most present-day children are just *starting* their education. He did, however, attend a night school in Hollinwood run by Primitive Methodists (Ranters) and also an "Owd Dame's School" on Wrigley Head, Failsworth - "penny a trip and bring your own candle" type of thing. Some readers may remember the Labour Club on Bower Lane, which was demolished about 1969. It was this building that was originally occupied by the Ranters and the pupils met in an upper room termed "The Old Garret". By 1828 there were so many scholars that the superintendent, James Schofield, found it necessary to move to Gravel Hole (now Bourne Street) just up the road, and it must have been this school that Ben attended.

Ben records that as a child he used to spend time watching the clogger's apprentices cross-cutting the elder (or "owler") timber for soles. He played at turning a handle in the Bower Lane rope walk until his hands were blistered all over, but when he was put to work on his father's bobbin wheel - "the twelve-legged boggart" - Ben detested the job. In an attempt to find a pleasant spot he would move the wheel around the house, on to the canal side or round the corner into Henfield Row ("Treadle-pin Fold") to watch the other children at play. But there was no escaping his father's shout of "Bobbins!" "Bobbins!" At one point Ben couldn't stand being left out of the other children's games any longer, so he turned his bobbin wheel upside down and trundled it round the fold shouting, "Sithors to grind!" ("Scissors sharpened!") Mr Brierley stepped out and wielded the empty shuttle with dexterity.

The row of canalside cottages at Hollinwood where Ben lived from the age of five

Ben wrote that they gave him up as "a bad job, so far as bobbin-winding was concerned" and he was sent to learn spinning in the factory. He doesn't say which factory but it was perhaps that of George Hinchcliffe, cotton spinner, since he admits to having worked there in "Ab o'th'Yate in Yankeeland". Ben became a little piecer, which involved reconnecting any broken threads. This is not hard work, as I can testify, but the speed of a gazelle and the eyesight of a hawk were required, as the frames ran at a speed just less than that which would make them invisible. And you couldn't tie any knots in the thread either! My time in the cotton mills of Chadderton in the 1970s was quite pleasantly spent, although the split-shift system of working *did* interfere with my drinking hours. But a century and a half earlier things were very different. Read Ben's first-hand report of what the mills were like in the 1830s and imagine what it was to go to work in such conditions...

"It was common enough to start the engine at half-past five, and not leave off until seven. The mills of that period were low, and badly ventilated. In some of them gas had not been introduced. In the one I worked at, candles were used, and were so scantily distributed as only to 'make darkness visible'." Those entering this gloomy atmosphere were not fortified by a warm bed and a cooked breakfast. Even if you can remember trying to light a coal fire on a cold morning in the days before central heating, you're not really close. Matches hadn't come into use yet "and the flint-and-steel was a luxury confined to the better-doing. If the house-fire had gone out at night we had no means of lighting it in the morning except by enclosing a candle in a home-made paper lantern, and going about the neighbourhood in search of an accessible fire. If none could be found at that early hour we had to encounter the severest weather, sometimes fasting, and often without having had anything warm... our constant companion being cold, darkness, and semi-starvation."

Wagstaff Fold, where Uncle Richard had his garden

Every cloud has a silver lining, though. One morning the mill manager noticed Ben reading in his breakfast half-hour. It turned out that he was perusing a copy of "Cleaves' Gazette", then published weekly and costing one penny, which he managed to save out of his threepence a fortnight "odd brass". The manager generously offered him the chance to read "The Pickwick Papers", which were at the time being published in serial form, if Ben would collect them from a nearby stationer's. I assume he agreed.

A combination of delicate health and poor working conditions forced Ben to leave the mill and for a time he went back to learn his trade on the hand-loom in his cottage by the canal. Whether he punced (kicked) his father off his board and installed himself, or whether he set up his own loom I can't say, but it was not uncommon to hear of a two- or even a four-loom house. Trade was often slack and the hand-loom weavers sometimes had to wait weeks for warps, and even longer for payment. When Ben had no other work, he employed himself in dragging a cart laden with coals from the Limeside workings for his neighbours - a distance of nearly a mile for a profit of threepence a round trip. This provided a meal for the family of four, who dined off two pennyworth of bacon and a pennyworth of potatoes. The shortage of work did give Ben time to pursue his other interests, though.

This drawing of "Pay Day in a Cotton Mill" gives some idea of the harsh conditions which people had to endure

Widening Horizons

At the tender age of sixteen our hero was acting as secretary to the "Mutual Improvement Society" he and his friends had established in "Th'owd Skoo" on Pole Lane. This later became the Mechanics' Institute, a *very* Victorian idea. They had no books to speak of, so they subscribed their pennies weekly until they had enough laid by to purchase some second-hand volumes. Ben's uncle, Richard Taylor, had taken a keen interest in their society and as he worked in Manchester, he was appointed to select a number of books from the second-hand bookshops there. Once selected and paid for, the volumes were collected by Ben and another eager beaver who set off walking to Manchester with a weaver's wallet to "bear whoam" their precious burden. The books were then covered with stout nankeen (a durable cotton cloth, usually yellow) to make them last for ever and a day. The area certainly wasn't short of weavers who could provide the material.

Uncle Richard had a garden in Wagstaff Fold, at the junction of what is now Kershaw Road and Ashton Road West (formerly Back Lane), and the group took to meeting there for "literary readings" on Sunday mornings. Later, the Failsworth Co-op was built on the site and the building is now occupied by Bickley's Carpets. For all his encouragement, Uncle Dick was not uncritical. It was he who had mocked Ben's childish habit of walking along with his hands behind his back, christening him "Owd Pee Colin", after a quaint character in the neighbourhood who had the same mannerism. Now Dick commented unfavourably on Ben's efforts in verse, saying that he thought "Owd Pee" would make more progress in weaving silk than he did in writing poetry.

Determined to prove to his well-read uncle that he *could* write acceptable verse, Ben set upon a plan. He persuaded his favourite companion, William Crossley, to write out one of Ben's efforts and present it to Uncle Dick for perusal. It was pronounced "Excellent, and well worthy of a place in the 'poets corner' of the newspapers." When the author's true name was revealed, Uncle Dick was astonished. "'And has Owd Pee really composed this poem? Well, I'll go to -!'" He had to admit that he had misjudged Ben's literary prowess. Not the first. Not the last.

Nevertheless, one of Ben's first known pieces of writing was entitled "My Uncle's Garden" and was written under his nom de plume of Saxon Wallbridge, a useful device when he began to make his name and met with the envious criticism of his fellows. His friend James Dronsfield, writing in 1896, said that this "served only to stimulate him to renewed energy, for he had a soul within him which soared above difficulties", or as Ben himself put it, "I had to make my own ladder before I could climb." It must have given him some fun if the following incident recounted by Dronsfield is anything to go by. James had been discussing with a mutual acquaintance an article by "Saxon Wallbridge" which had appeared in the Manchester Spectator and the acquaintance had pronounced it the best sketch in Lancashire dialect he had ever read, concluding, "If I were Ben Brierley I would never again venture as a Lancashire writer because he cannot compare with Saxon Wallbridge." When Dronsfield explained that he thought Ben and Mr Wallbridge were one and the same, the critic walked away shaking his head, but soon had to admit he was wrong. Ben's reaction when challenged on the matter was typical of him: "He seemed rather reticent at first, but I noticed a faint smile on his countenance when I began to beat about the bush for information. At length I ventured to enquire if Saxon Wallbridge was any relation of Ben Brierley's. His smile was soon transformed into a hearty laugh, and he replied, 'Gex agen an' theau'll happen be fur off th'mark.'"

As Ben grew up, he naturally became interested in politics. His father had been at Peterloo in 1819 and had taken part in the Radical agitation which resulted in the First Reform Act of 1832. This removed some of the worst inequalities of the political system. For example, before the Act, Old Sarum, an ancient earthwork occupied by only a handful of people, had two MPs, while the rapidly growing town of Manchester had none! But many anomalies remained and the Act still gave less than 30% of the population the right to vote. The People's Charter, published in

There were several Chartist meetings on Granby Row Fields, Manchester, in 1842. Possibly this drawing depicts the one on 11th August, when the Mayor arrived to read the Riot Act and brought in troops to disperse the crowds. Even the liberal Manchester Guardian referred to the rioters as "a gang of desperate and unprincipled agitators".

1838, "requested and required" an equal number of voters in constituencies, annual general elections (God forbid!), universal manhood suffrage, vote by secret ballot, abolition of land qualifications for prospective Parliamentary candidates and payment for MPs (so that even a poor man might attend). The Chartist movement grew and the rejection of a second petition to Parliament in 1842, combined with bad trade and wage reductions locally, led to a series of strikes centred on places like Ashton, Failsworth and Hollinwood in the August of that year. They became known as the "Plug Riots" because they involved groups of workers going round the large mills of the time and extracting the drain plugs from the boilers, thereby halting production. Ben was involved and narrowly escaped arrest as a result of his activities.

Having done his bit, he didn't find it inconsistent to return to work at his loom and he did quite well for a time reeling off velvet - the strikes had increased the price by twenty percent!

For a time he was able to do more than work and at some point during these years he returned to "Th'owd Skoo" on Pole Lane as a Sunday teacher. When Ben went there as a child it was inter-denominational, but he records that the Church Party later became dominant and in 1837 built their own school. "Social dissensions quickly followed the separation of that party from the mother establishment," wrote Ben. They were soon to escalate into open warfare, when the old building became "a bone of contention betwixt the Church Party and the 'Anythinarians'". But for the time being, as already mentioned, the Pole Lane premises became the home of the Mutual Improvement Society and "the poor man's college".

As well as teaching each other the basics of reading and writing, they made their own entertainment. The old building must have been packed to bursting point as "Othello", "Hamlet", "Wat Tyler" and "The Bleeding Nun" were acted out with great gusto, but while they were *playing*, they were *learning*. It was here that Ben made his first stage appearance, in "Ducks and Peas, or the Newcastle Rider". Apparently he was much obsessed with tragedy in his younger days and took to wearing a tie like Lord Byron's and cultivating the melancholy to go with it. This side of his character seems to have been reflected in his play, "Marinello the Monk", which was offered at Pole Lane to a sombre audience. As well as writing the piece, Ben starred as the villain. It must have been an effective performance, for his sweetheart of the time came up to him after the curtain fell, looked him straight in the eye and said she would have nothing more to say to "sich a bad un as thee." Perhaps this was the best lesson Ben ever learned at "Th'owd Skoo".

The Old School, from a drawing by Thomas Anderton

Another person who was not well pleased with the goings-on was the newly-appointed Rector of St John's. In Failsworth's case, the church school preceded the church, the foundation stone of which was laid in 1845 by Harry Walmsley, a member of a prominent local family.

Harry was the eldest son of Thomas Walmsley, who, along with his brother Joseph, migrated to Failsworth from Bacup at the beginning of the nineteenth century. What attracted the brothers to the area were the possibilities presented by the making of the Rochdale Canal, which passed under the highway from Manchester to Oldham not many yards from where Ben was born. Thomas got there in time to cater for the gangs of navvies who built the canal as well as those who used the completed waterway, and he seized the opportunity to build a house, corn warehouse and grocer's shop adjoining the bridge. Thus the approach from the Manchester side became known as Walmsley Brow and the bridge itself as Walmsley Bridge. Within thirty years Thomas had amassed enough capital to erect and equip Firs Mill, later known as Gladstone Mill. The mill was opened in 1839 and enlarged six years later; by this time seven hundred people worked there, and most of them bought their provisions from Walmsley's shop, or Mr W wanted to know the reason why not! Thomas placed the mill under the management of Harry and the grocery side in the less capable hands of Jonathan, his younger son.

1845 was a significant year in the annals of Failsworth and of the Walmsleys. The factory was enlarged, Harry laid the foundation stone of St John's and he also snapped up the lease of the land on which "Th'owd Skoo" was built. Thus began a long-running dispute in which Ben was intimately involved.

The master of the day school, John Goodier, had died and a successor was elected, but the Church Party, who disapproved of the amateur dramatics at the Old School, attempted to stop the activities there. Harry wanted to sell the building and his men seized the lower schoolroom and fastened up the door, but they had to leave the door communicating with the schoolhouse open as John Goodier's widow was still living there. Ben and his friends were determined to retake the building, but it was not a simple task: "A watchman held nightly ward in the schoolhouse, and had foiled several attempts on our part to make a lodgement in the beleaguered room. To get this official out of the way... was the chief point to be aimed at... Fortunately he was not a teetotaller... A passive sympathiser with our cause, who was in the habit of frequenting the enemy's camp, plied the two-legged 'Cerberus' with plentiful potations, and got him in such a state of obliviousness, that when the hour of attack presented itself, lo, 'the watch slumbered and slept'."

That Saturday evening one of Ben's chums produced a joiner's brace and bit and began boring one of the boards in the floor of the schoolhouse, which was above the schoolroom. ("The noise of a saw might have betrayed our purpose" - not numb, that lot!) Then came the question, "Neaw, then, who's for goin' deawn?... Leet weights preferred." A rope was drawn out of the coalhole and Ben found himself suspended with his clogs dangling through the hole. "I was the first let down. The duty assigned to me was to secure the door communicating with the schoolhouse... This I made right by passing a cord several times through the door handle and round a cross-wood of reliable strength." The others joined him and "The section of board was quickly replaced in the floor, and smeared over with dust... What consternation there was in our opponents' camp when it became known that business was being carried on in the lower school-room as if it had never been at all interrupted."

As part of the campaign, Ben wrote a song several verses long poking fun at "Lord Harry" and arranged for copies to be pinned up in prominent positions around the township. The friction between them increased to such a point that Walmsley summonsed him, but authorship could not be proven (Ben wasn't daft enough to sign it) and although he was caught with a copy in his hands and taken to court, an apology from his solicitor (not Ben himself!) was accepted and the matter was grudgingly dropped. Even from this verse, one can see why Harry Walmsley was annoyed:

My name is Lord Harry the Slasher,
And I live at the Pinch-Beggars Hall,
At the doors I'm a regular smasher,
And banditti I have at my call.
I'm a dread to the lads, I assure you,
And oft their brave spirits I quell;
They will take to their heels in a fury,
When they hear of Lord Harry the Swell.

Chorus:
Then hurrah for Lord Harry the Swell,
I'm a foe to all that the lads do,
While my name is Lord Harry the Swell.

"Slasher", I assume, was a reference to the fact that Harry was forever cutting the wages of his workers on one pretext or another. Ben's attitude was that respect had to be earned over a long period, not just asked for and got; otherwise it becomes subservience, and Ben would have none of that!

In the end, the people of Failsworth were victorious and the Old School remained; in 1880 it was replaced by a second "Old School" on the same site. Fittingly, on Saturday, 27th June 1925, a Ben Brierley Celebration was held in the Secular Schoolroom, the predecessor of which he had done so much to preserve. A souvenir programme sold for twopence reveals that the Chairman's Address was given by Councillor William Dunkerley, Chairman of Failsworth District Council, and that there were several readings of Ben's works and performances of at least ten songs written by Brierley, Laycock or Waugh, accompanied by Miss Ida Beech on piano. If this wasn't enough, two selected songs were crooned by Mr R Brierley and a brief address given by Dr Henry Brierley, B.A, after the interval. The festival was rounded off by the singing of the National Anthem. I'm sure a good time was had by all.

For the last fifteen years of its useful life, from Easter 1970 to November 1985, the second school

Firs Hall

was used by the Jehovah's Witnesses as their Kingdom Hall. Shortly afterwards the building was demolished and the site of the Old Schools is now covered by a block of four maisonettes.

Perhaps it would have been some consolation to Harry Walmsley to know that his warehouse outlasted the Old School and still stands, as does the family's home, Firs Hall, built in the mid-nineteenth century. St John's Church is still there too, now boasting a spire which was added in 1879. Will the shades of Lord Harry and the Rector appear at the Ben Brierley celebrations planned for 1996? I wonder.

Manchester and Marriage

These were lively times in national as well as local politics and Ben remembered his next employment as starting "the day following the public rejoicings on the occasion of the repeal of the Corn Laws". (These laws, designed to protect British agriculture by restricting the import of grain, often contributed towards high food prices and were much disliked. They were repealed in 1846.) The job was in the silk warehouse of J T & T Walker in York Street, Manchester, where an uncle was manager. Ben was twenty-one at the time and we must assume that the uncle suffered from nepotism.

The Suicide

Upon a rock which overhung a stream
A lovely maiden stood. Upon her cheek,
Which once the smiles of love and hope adorned,
Despair had laid its cold and blighting hand.
Her face was shaded by a row of curls,
Which hung like mourning cherubs o'er her brow,
Seeming to take a lingering farewell look
Of her sweet eyes which like two sister nymphs
Sat in their bowers weeping themselves away;
She stood like one whose earthly joys had fled,
And all her hopes of heaven had met their grave,
Mute, still, and thoughtful, gazing on the flood.

All nature smiled and wore the garb of joy,
The trees waved forth in verdant liveliness,
And flowers refreshed with dews smiled at the sun;
But neither tree nor flower engaged her sight.
The wanton kine were leaping on the brows,
And sportive lambs were frisking in the vale;
But still she seemed as though she saw them not,
Or heeded not their gambols if she did.
The sabbath bells awoke their morning peal,
Which, mingling with the songs of sylvan choirs,
Produced a sweet harmonious melody;
But then her ear, once music's heaven, was shut
To such sweet sounds as kindle thoughts of love
And make our senses wander to the skies.

The bells had ceased, all nature seemed to pause;
A breathless stillness reigned within the woods.
She press'd her hands in silence to her breast-
She raised her eyes imploringly to heaven,
She breathed a prayer, it was for him she loved,
Who had betrayed and left her to her fate,
She waved her hand which seemed to say "I come,"
She leaped - she fell - she shrieked - she was no more,
Her heart was broken and her soul was gone.

John Bolton Rogerson

It was during his dinner break from the silk mill that Ben came into contact with somebody else who was to come in useful: Elijah Ridings, who had a second-hand bookstall on the footpath opposite the Seven Stars in Withy Grove. Elijah had also been born in Failsworth - in 1802 - and in his early days had been a hand-loom weaver but one who, like Ben, read extensively in his spare time. He had attended Peterloo with Ben's father in 1819 and later had much to do with Manchester's petition in favour of the Reform Bill. It appears that he did a spell in Lancaster jail for debt in the 1830s, but got back on his feet again and entered the book trade, running a shop on Lower King Street as well as the stall on Withy Grove. His poetry became popular from the 1840s onward, perhaps his most famous collection being "The Village Muse". He was laid to rest in Harpurhey General Cemetery in 1872 and Ben was interred not many yards from him a quarter of a century later. But back to the 1840s and Ben's dinner break.

He visited the bookstall often enough to get on chatting terms with Elijah and later wrote down his recollections of how the acquaintance developed:

"Seeing that I was a country lad he began to ask me questions about my 'come fro'; and I was only too delighted to give him all the information I could.

'Ay, an' art thou James Breerley lad,' Elijah exclaimed, after I had given him 'the story of my life from year to year'. 'Well, then thy mother would be Esther Whitehead?' I told him that was my mother's maiden name. 'Ay, ay, I knew her. Hoo used to sing under my feyther at Newton Church. Ax her if hoo knew owd Jim Ridings. Here's a book o' mine I'll gie thee, an' I'll put my name in it.'"

Ben was encouraged by this kindness to show Elijah some of his work and reported a favourable reception: "'An' has thou written this?' he asked, when he had read the scrap. I owned, with not a little pride, that I was responsible for its production. 'Here, I'll gie thee a note to John Bolton Rogerson. He's th'editor o'th'Oddfellows' Magazine; an' his office is i' Dale Street.'" John Bolton Rogerson, born in Manchester in 1809 and like Ben an avid reader since childhood, well knew how difficult it was for a young writer to get into print. Twenty years earlier he had had his own first poem, "The Farewell", published in the Manchester Guardian and went on to edit several short-lived literary publications before leaving his position as a solicitor's clerk to become a bookseller. He joined the Oddfellows in 1838 and began editing the quarterly magazine in 1841.

Ben was kindly received and his poem appeared in the next issue, the first time he had seen his name in print. And so "the old poet" (Elijah was in his forties!) gave Ben "A Lift on the Way", to quote Waugh. He inspired him in other ways, too. Once Ben was lamenting that he couldn't afford to buy a book and Elijah said to him, "If I'd fifty pounds I'd go to Lunnon, an' buy a ton o'books." "What a magnificent spectacle this presented to me!" wrote Ben, and someone else commented, "What a boon and a blessing it would be to all young people if they could only look on books in the same light as Ben and Elijah, instead of spending their precious time and money in reading the scrappy stuff of the present day!"

That first poem, "The Suicide", appeared in July 1846 and is reproduced on page 10. "To Death" followed in October and "The Voice of Memory" in January 1847. Well, I said Ben was obsessed with tragedy! Perhaps Rogerson advised him to cheer his work up a bit, for "Song of a Mountaineer" (below) in the April issue was still dark and dramatic in its atmosphere, but a bit more lively.

Ben and Elijah never received the recognition that they deserved. A house that Ben would have known well from the outside was Failsworth Lodge (Birch Villa, the Lancaster Club, Avro Sports Club, British Aerospace Club, call it what you will). A large car boot sale is held there every Sunday morning and at one of these I was able to pick up an 1881 copy of "Ab o'th'Yate's Dictionary" for fifty pence! Ben's name is mentioned nowhere in the volume, not even in the copyright declaration!

The grounds of Failsworth Lodge and the reclaimed land on the banks of Moston Brook provide great sport for my overweight dog, 'Ben Brierley', as he pursues rabbits in a pathetic attempt to appear agile. The real Ben Brierley, somewhat fitter, would have passed the house on his daily trek from Hollinwood to his job in the Manchester silk mill and passed it again on the way back. Today it is all Oldham Road, but then the four-and-a-half-mile stretch changed its name along its length: Watchcote, Dob Lane, Newton Lane. Ben went on foot because there were no omnibuses to catch, and even if there had been, no doubt he would have been unable or unwilling to pay for the pleasure of being jerked about here, there and everywhere on a rough road. But "whilst mornings were fine and winter not too near" there were compensations: "From sallying out from home at half-past six I could have a good hour's reading on the road."

He certainly wouldn't have bumped into any lamp posts as he walked through Failsworth, as these refinements were not adopted until a *very* late date, hence the name "Darktown". Now let's see: Ben did this journey from Hollinwood to Manchester and back again for nine years. Assuming a few holidays here and there and Sundays off, that makes a grand total of some 20,000 miles! It's a wonder he had any time for literary work, but he did.

In the May of 1854 Ben was on his way home when he stopped at a

Song of a Mountaineer

Away ye gay and shady bowers,
Ye bright and sunny vales!
Where perfume springs from fragrant flowers,
And sweetly scents the gales.
Give me the hills, the towering hills,
Where tempests loudly roar;
For I'm a child of the mountains wild,
And my home is on the moor.

I love to climb the craggy steep
When thunders shake the air,
When dreary glens, and caverns deep,
Are lit by the lightning's glare;
I love to view the torrents blue,
As they lash the shaking shore;
For I'm a child of the mountains wild,
And my home is on the moor.

I hear no voice but the voice of God,
As it thunders in the storm;
I dread no power but his mighty rod,
When it mars the mountain's form;
Oft do I sleep on the storm-rock'd steep,
While the clouds are rushing o'er;
For I'm a child of the mountains wild,
And my home is on the moor.

horse trough outside a public house in Miles Platting for a quick swill and heard a "layrock" (lark) singing overhead. He decided there and then to compose a tribute to the time of year and with the renowned Brierley flair, titled it "May-Day". He sent a copy to the Manchester Guardian, which was published bi-weekly then, and it appeared in the next issue. If nothing else, it proved that Ben could write in standard English as well as in the Lancashire dialect. He didn't forget his "layrock":

Drinking ether as he sings,
Flashing sunlight from his wings,
The soaring lark, with merry throat,
Warbles shrill his 'Maying' note.

Back to the warping rooom of J T & T Walker in York Street. Over it there worked a girl "with light wavy hair, and a face upon which Honesty had put its stamp." Her name was Esther Firth and she hailed from Bowlee Heights. One evening as they were leaving the warehouse, Ben made up his mind

"Sober" Job Ogden and his wife; a photograph taken in the 1880s

to speak to her. "Thou'll get bagged [sacked] ift'does," said a shopmate, as they followed behind the girl and her companions. "I'll risk being 'bagged'," he said, although his uncle was very strict about such matters. He spoke to her - no doubt some inconsequential drivel, but enough to find out her Christian name. Now Ben's mother, Esther Whitehead, died in the autumn of 1854 and he later claimed to have vowed never to marry unless he met a girl with the same virtues and name as his mother (though to be fair, Ben was a master at squeezing a story out of a coincidence and turning it into a tall tale). Whether it was coincidence or not, his fate was sealed and many years later he reported, "I have not yet lived to deplore the circumstances in which we first met." They were married at Manchester Cathedral on 29th April 1855, when Ben was nearly thirty.

Shortly beforehand his uncle, the works manager, died and the wedding present from his employers was to give him the sack, or in weaving parlance to "make up his book", so that he was out of work for ten weeks. He managed to get a start in a silk warehouse owned by Brotherton & Green in Fountain Street, where he worked until nine o'clock every night during the week and until ten o'clock on Saturdays. During Ben's time here, a holiday was called celebrating the fall of Sebastopol (September 1855) and it was then that he formed the idea of writing "A Day Out", his first prose of any note. The content was effectively summarised by James Middleton as "a simple description of a walk, probably from the Bradford side of Manchester City by the river [Medlock], through the fields, along the brookside, through the cloughs, on to the secluded nook which has lived on daisies ever since."

"A Day Out" was to have quite an effect on Ben's fortunes, but for the moment he found himself looking for a new job as trade slackened. He moved to Messrs Brennan & Sons in Church Street, working with silk again.

Ben and Esther's only child,

James Dronsfield, from a painting by W H Wimpenny

Annie, was born in 1856 and by the time she was two they were living in Whitley Street, Collyhurst, off St George's Road (now Rochdale Road). They were to stay in the district, in different houses, for almost thirty years.

Ben used to conceal the identity of the *very real* places he was writing about by giving them slightly different names, only recognisable by the folk who lived there: "Hazelworth", for example, was Failsworth, "Mossburn" Moston, "Merriton" Middleton and so on. "Bardsley Fold" became "Walmsley Fowt" in his writings, and let's have one thing clear: Ben Brierley, who was known as Ab o'th'Yate, never lived there. His model for "Ab", Job Ogden, did (there is an Ogden Road in the locality which may or may not be named after him).

Was the choice of the name "Walmsley Fowt" a dig at his old adversary, Harry Walmsley? In 1858, Harry "came at variance" with his weavers. The reason they "varied" was that Harry had speeded up some of the looms and then offered a reduction in wages of from twopence to fourpence a cut. The bitter dispute ended by him throwing out all his looms, and presumably the weavers as well, and installing additional spinning frames in the space vacated. Although he never actually worked for Walmsleys, Ben wasn't too happy with the state of affairs and it may have given him pleasure to realise that on this occasion there was little Harry could do about the veiled reference to him.

It wasn't just personal animosity, for Mr Walmsley does seem to have had a general reputation for meanness. The first Failsworth Pole blew down on 7th October 1849 and the second was a ship's mainmast 78 feet long and 20 inches in diameter. Elijah Ridings, who could not be accused of being an angry young man by then, commented drily that the second pole was erected "at the direction of, if not at the expense of, Harry Walmsley".

Dronsfield and Bamford

It was during this period that Ben was introduced to that sturdy old Radical and writer, Samuel Bamford, who was almost forty years his senior, having been born in Middleton in 1788. It was a relationship that was to last until Sam was laid to rest in Middleton Churchyard. Sam Bamford's monument stands not far from his grave, overlooking the town, and *stand* it does! It is a stone needle eight yards high. I've never seen anything like it in my life!

By contrast, Sam's home in Hall Street, Moston, where Ben was introduced to him, was described as a "small cottage". Ben removed to number 17 in the same street about fifteen years after Sam's death, to a house pompously called "The Poplars", and having seen a photograph of this, I dread to think how tiny the "small cottage" must have been. Sam and Ben had certainly met by 1858, soon after Sam's return from a stay in the capital, for Sam's diary for 25th September that year records a visit to Brierley's, adjourned to the Cloggers Arms, where he "heard more real, thoughtful expression in the course of half an hour, than [he] had done amongst working men in London during seven years." Ben would have known *of* the old reformer from his childhood, but the introduction was made by James Dronsfield, later to write for the Oldham Chronicle under the pseudonym of Jerry Lichenmoss.

Just to make the picture a little clearer, I'll say a word or two about James Dronsfield. Born in Hollinwood on 21st January 1826, he died in Oldham six months after Ben, on 24th June 1896. James's parents deemed it best for his future well-being if he learnt a trade and for this purpose he was bound apprentice to a blacksmith in Blackley. While there, he often saw the manly figure of Sam Bamford striding along Valentine Brow and at length ventured to speak to him. Another friendship was formed

Samuel Bamford

that was to last until the grave, and indeed James was present at Sam's death.

About 1856 James went into business as a blacksmith on his own account in his native village of Hollinwood, his smithy being at the junction of Chapel Road and Chamber Road with Manchester Road. After retiring from this, he became an outdoor superintendent of gas and water mains for Oldham Corporation. He was a born humorist and contributed articles to the Oldham Co-operative Record, among other publications, and some of these were collected and issued as "Ouselwood" after his death. No more worthy and fitting tribute could have been paid to him than the pressing request that he should edit the special publication of Ben Brierley's three-volume set of "Ab o'th'Yate Sketches" put out by W E Clegg of Oldham in 1896, just after Ben's death. Sadly, James himself died just short of completing the task, the final few proofs being read by his son John and Mr Charles Walters - whoever he might be.

James Dronsfield is buried in the churchyard of St Margaret's, Hollinwood, his stone being one of the few left standing after the graveyard was grassed over. He lies with his wife, Ann, who passed away in 1893 and his little

Henfield Row, Hollinwood, the model for "Treadle-pin Fowt"

son Bamford - named after Sam - who died in May 1861.

By the time Ben met him, Sam Bamford was a little "over the hill", though nobody told him so to his face, I suspect! Ben used to accompany him when they gave readings of their works and it was quite common for the younger man to take over and "carry" Sam, for age wasn't on his side and he spoke with a broad Lancashire accent and a slight stutter, which got worse and worse as he became more agitated. Ben recalled that at one performance Sam was reading from a new copy of his book and turned over a page that wasn't cut - in effect, two pages at once. He failed to realise what was the matter and began flicking the pages this way and that in a vain effort to regain the thread. By this time the assembly was in an uproar and that only made Sam's stutter worse.

When Ben did help, Sam wasn't a bit grateful! Of a joint performance they did in 1859, he commented gruffly that Ben's reading was "not any additional attraction" - but he did worry that he'd hurt Ben's feelings and tried to make amends. In August 1860 Ben, Dronsfield and a few other friends including Sam went on a trip to Stalybridge, which was partly a wasted journey because the man they had gone to see was out. The day ended up as a pub crawl with a fair bit of walking in between and Sam was tired out: "Damn all such pleasure trips, say I," he wrote, while at the same time being concerned that he'd spoilt their fun. With an old man's caution, he fretted about Ben when he gave up his job as a warper at Brennan & Sons in 1861: "I am afraid he is getting into a loose way and acting wildly."

An engraving based on Charles Potter's "Daisy Nook"

On the other hand, Sam accepted loans of much-needed money and Ben looked after his well-being in general - they were very close. But they didn't always see eye to eye, disagreeing over the most trivial thing and arguing as only friends can, without animosity and tongue in cheek. A good instance of this would be Sam's mode of setting the Lancashire dialect on to paper: "I had many a tiff with him, but he always worsted me by asserting his right to do what he liked with his own property. He would often get in a passion, and did not care what he said at such times."

Regarding Sam's poem "My Wynder" (a person who winds bobbins), Ben suggested as they were revising it for publication that "i" would be a better spelling than "y", since it gave the same sound both in the dialect and in proper English. "'It does be d----d as like!' Sam exclaimed with plenty of warmth. 'W-i-n-d-e-r would be *winder*,' he said, sounding the *i* as in *window*. 'An' if theau spells it that way I'll bag thee!'" Ben gave in! And I think Sam was right, for "wynder" is a perfect rhyme for "join'd her", which would have been pronounced "jind'er" in the dialect.

As it happens, Sam didn't write in the dialect very much, but Ben *did*! If you compare "A Day Out" of 1856, published by John Heywood, with the revised version published by his brother Abel a year or two later, it will be discovered that most of the dialect words have been toned down in the later edition to appeal to a wider reading public. For example, "an goo up owd Mattheaw Keaw Loane" becomes "an' goo up owd Mattheaw Cow Lone", and "abeaut two eawnces a week" is "about two ounces a week" in the later version. Similarly, the sketch "Treadlepin Fold" in Abel Heywood's version is called "Traddlepin Fold" throughout John Heywood's publication. Surprisingly, though, the "harder" dialect version of Ben's "Ab o'th'Yate Sketches" appears in the W B Clegg volumes published in 1896, although Ben rewrote many of them for publication in his "Journal" some years earlier.

Variations such as "Theaw", "Theau", "Thou" and so on aren't always as random as they seem, and must be taken in context. In Ben's tale of the Stuffed Monkey (Boggart o'th'Stump) the auctioneer is made to speak in the Ashton variant of the Lancashire dialect. Robert Dottie's "Rambles and Recollections" of 1898 uses the Bolton variety, and these have been clearly identified by people who know. This author contributed articles to Ben Brierley's Journal under the name of "R Dick", and "RP", who wrote the preface to Robert Dottie's book, covers the age-old problem of attempting to set a sound on to paper rather well. Much of what he says applies equally to Ben's works: "The author is the best one to look after his own spelling, phonetic or otherwise... The Lancashire dialect is not always of uniform breadth in the same individual. It is generally as broad as it's long, but sometimes broader. And when on his best behaviour - speaking to a Duke, for instance - his vernacular, contrariwise, often becomes little more than ordinary English - *with an accent*... The reader is respectfully desired to consider this, if, in the following pages, he finds the same words spelled two or three different ways, it is not through carelessness, but rather conscientiousness, and done of malice aforethought." So there.

Back to the relationship between Ben Brierley and Sam Bamford. An anecdote recorded in Ben's "Home Memories" illustrates the fact that they were always at each other's throats - with a feather. They had been invited to a literary dinner by the Mayor of Manchester, John Grave. Sam was over eighty then and the Mayor sent his carriage with instructions that Ben should bring him to Mount House, Cheetham, whether the old reformer objected or not: "I had much difficulty in executing my commission, meeting with rebuffs of no very pleasant character. *He* was not going to be taken like a 'madman' with a 'keeper'. He knew his way, and could walk it. We agreed at last to reverse matters, he must take me; so with that understanding I got him into the carriage, and drove to Mount House." Ben had planned to drop Sam off on his way home, but the old fellow outwitted him. "Without acquainting me with his intentions he landed me at my own door, which was attended to by my wife. 'Here, missis,' he said, 'I've browt this lad o'yor's whoam.' Then with a chuckle he drove off."

When Sam died on 13th April 1872, Ben wrote an appreciation of him. Three years later the similarities between them were brought home in particularly poignant circumstances and a long time afterwards Ben looked back on events like this: "Bamford's great misfortune, the loss of his only child in her early womanhood, always impressed me with a painful feeling, because I had a presentiment that such would be my lot. I had my only one - bearing the same Christian name. We had both been hand-loom weavers, and shared poverty alike. The affinity of every circumstance appalled me whenever the idea crossed my mind... The blow came at last. In her nineteenth year ours was taken from us."

But I'm getting ahead of myself again...

A Literary Career

In the early 1860s Ben was offered a post as sub-editor for the Oldham Times, thanks to the influence of a friend, Charles Potter, who was then struggling to make his mark as an artist. Ben commissioned Potter to draw a vignette depicting Daisy Nook, to be used in conjunction with "A Day Out", but when asked where Daisy Nook was, Ben replied, "I've no particular place; theaw con fix it where theaw likes." So Mr Potter set up his easel in the picturesque village of Waterhouses, by the River Medlock at the Droylsden end of Failsworth and captured for all time the spot which to this very day is called "Daisy Nook". It was an ideal choice, judging by the description of the hostelry there in Jane Taylor's "Frozen Music": "A 17th century limewashed brown brick building with later alterations. The datestone is engraved 16.., and it is said to have been occupied by Miles and Margaret Bouldes in 1608... The interior has hewn bevelled beams. Red Bill's used to be the Medlock Tavern, and acquired its present name when the landlord, Nat Spencer, [who owned a three-legged bulldog, I believe] posed for Charles Potter's

Red Bill's, Daisy Nook, in the 1880s

painting." Why "Red Bill's" and not "Red Nat's"? Well, Ben called his landlord William Simister.

So successful were Ben's "Daisy Nook Sketches" that sleepy Waterhouses was transformed almost overnight into a mini-Blackpool. People from the surrounding towns and villages flocked there for "A Day Out", no doubt hoping to catch a glimpse of Ab himself. The local yokels were not slow in cashing in on the boom. Some cottages became tea-shops offering refreshments, at others you could get hot water to brew your own, and a bandstand and dancing boards (one almost sixty feet long) sprang up. The Woodhouses Reed Band played and the clog-shod visitors tripped the "heavy fantastic". A Ben Brierley terrace appeared, complete with wooden tea-shop at one end; each of its three entrances was named after one of Ben's characters - Sam o'Ducky's, Fause Juddie and Jack o'Flunter's. While "Owd Ab's" provided tea, clicking was to be heard from a multitude of photographic booths providing memories, and it was computed that on Good Friday 1900, more than forty years after the place became identified with Daisy Nook, "No less than 80,000 people arrived, some of them from a considerable distance." "Red Bill's" closed as a pub in 1936 and I believe that "Owd Ab's" was demolished three months before the onset of the Second World War, the terrace surviving for another twenty years or more.

Ben kept up his acquaintance with John Bolton Rogerson, the editor of the Oddfellows Magazine, and this proved useful to him in more ways than one, for it was at a soirée given by Rogerson that he first met Edwin Waugh. They became friends and Waugh in turn introduced him to the editor of the Manchester Weekly Times, Henry Barry Peacock. Ben was grateful, for much of his early work appeared in the Weekly Times in serial form, including "Irkdale" or "The Odd House in the Hollow", subsequently published in two volumes by Messrs Tinsley Brothers of London. I'm not surprised it took two volumes, for in one it is an ungainly beast and although it is really several stories intertwined and some interesting characters are introduced, it could be termed "Irksome" by those who prefer his shorter, snappier sketches.

In 1862 Ben left his post at the Oldham Times, having obtained a short engagement in London. While there he was introduced to the Savage Club and made the acquaintance of some of the dramatic celebrities of the time: the Brough brothers, Andrew Halliday and T W Robertson, among others. When Colman's Magazine, which had been started by members of the club, collapsed, Ben returned to Manchester. "The Layrock of Langleyside" first appeared in serialised form in Colman's, to be completed in the Manchester Weekly Times after his return home. So the good people of Manchester got to know that "the butler did it", but did *what* was left to their imaginations, it seems! The whole thing was later published in book form with a frontispiece by Charles Potter. Other works first serialised in the Weekly Times were "Red Windows Hall", "The Fratchingtons of Fratchingthorpe" and "Ab o'th'Yate on Times and Things".

The Failsworth Industrial Society gave an annual tea party in Culcheth Schools, Newton Heath, and it is recorded that on one of these occasions the entertainment consisted solely of Ben's "Fratchingtons of Fratchingthorpe", performed by Thomas Taylor and Miss M A Barton. I would love to have been there, ignoring the tea, to witness it! The sketch involves Tim and Peggy frapping (arguing) their way through five fraps, consisting of many pages of dialogue. This may sound boring, but having read it and mastered the dialogue, I have come to the conclusion that it is one of the wittiest pieces that Ben ever wrote. He certainly suffered from keen observation, if nothing else!

"Peggy Fratchington has just found out what makes her husband, Timothy Fratchington, stop so late at the 'Brown Cow', when he ought to have been somewhere else. Timothy... after 'roasting his shins' several hours at the kitchen-fire of his favourite tavern, comes home with 'a gradely looad on'; or rather, in that state of physical and mental incapacity which in polite phraseology would be termed 'tightly screwed'. Peggy, who has been 'gathering her brows like gathering storm - nursing her wrath to keep it warm', has just attained that degree of mental serenity and amiableness of disposition which makes the domestic hearth rather too warm to be comfortable, and consequently has laid aside her knitting in order to give more freedom to the action of her nails." The outcome need not be discussed here!

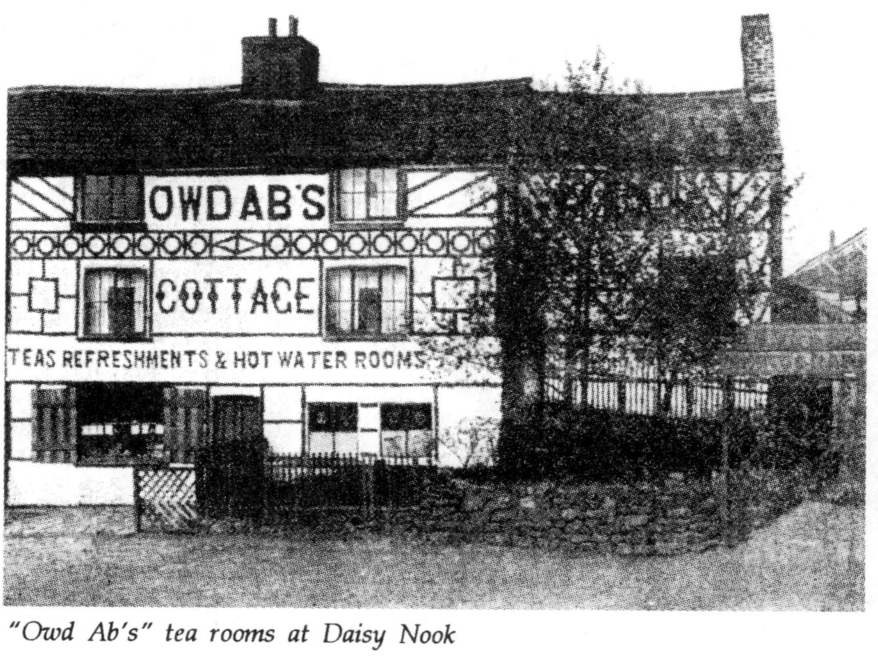

"Owd Ab's" tea rooms at Daisy Nook

The writing of the "Daisy Nook Sketches" gave Ben entrée into the social and literary circle of people who occasionally gathered in the coffee room of the Clarence Hotel in Spring Gardens, Manchester. This circle of friends eventually became known as the Manchester Literary Club and among its members were Edwin Waugh, Charles Hardwick, Richard Rome Bealey, Charles Swain, John Harland, T T Wilkinson, David Morris and J P Stokes. Their first meetings were at the Cathedral Hotel, kept at the time by Mr D T Batty, but the club did move about from place to place.

Despite his considerable literary output, Ben still found time to get out and about and to do "research" at first hand. On 10th February 1902, Mr Thomas Newbigging read a paper to the Manchester Literary Society, reminiscing about Ben as he was in the 1860s. Thomas Newbigging was quite a character in his own right. Born in Glasgow in 1833, he moved with his family to Lancashire and by 1851 was living at Newchurch-in-Rossendale. He became known as "The Rossendale Writer" and was a *very* clever man. At the age of twenty-four he was appointed manager of the local gas company and in the 1870s went out to Brazil to manage a gas works there. For his services to that country he was created a Knight of the Order of the Rose. He returned to Manchester in 1875 and in addition to his business and political activities became a prolific author, not only of technical works on gas, but also in both his Scottish vernacular and in the Lancashire dialect. He also became Vice-President of Manchester Literary Club, which brings me back to what he had to say about Mr Brierley: "Ben was a bright, smart fellow then, of about forty, with an old-young face, florid complexion, sandy hair, thin but wiry in build, dapper and rather natty and genteel in appearance." Ben had been invited by Newbigging to Bacup early in 1864 to give readings from his "Lancashire Sketches" and "In the course of the evening Ben expressed a strong desire to visit the source of the River Irwell, and I, being well familiar with the hills all round the locality, willingly agreed to be his cicerone... We soon found the main Spring... Its surface was frozen over, but a slender thread of water issued from one side. I broke the ice with a stone, and expressing regret that we had not a walking-stick with us... by which we might have gauged the depth of the well, Ben suggested that I should use my leg for that purpose, a suggestion I respectfully declined to adopt... After satisfying our quest, I proposed that we should adjourn to the Dirplay Inn... On asking Ben what his special weakness by way of refreshment was,
'Hey missis,' said he to the landlady, 'Han yo' ony new milk? I know yo' han a stock o' rum.'
'Yei, maister,' was the response, 'we han boath new milk and rum.'
'Then bring us a quart to be going on wi',' said Ben...

There could be no manner of doubt that new milk and rum was Ben's special weakness." Hence, presumably, the florid complexion (the same as mine, but I miss out the milk). Well, Ben did once call milk and rum "The Milk o' Paradise" and the picture of him

The Unitarian Chapel at Stand; Ben lived at the Parsonage for a time in the 1860s

given by Mr Newbigging seems to me entirely credible, except for one small comment. Harking back to their discovery of the spring which gave rise to the Irwell, he said he thought Ben was not impressed by the source. "But imagination was not Ben's strong point." I should have thought the opposite were true.

While Ben was writing "Irkdale", when his daughter Annie was about nine, the family was invited to spend a few months at the Unitarian Parsonage at Stand while the pastor and his family travelled on the Continent. Ben recalled this episode in his life with pleasure, for among other things he was a neighbour of Richard Rome Bealey, author of "After Business Jottings" and other poems. Bealey was a Freemason and his "The Man who is Kind to Another" was sung many times at Masonic installations as "The Master's Song". It may well have been his influence which led to Ben being initiated on St Valentine's Day 1865 in Merit Lodge, which then met on the Tuesday after each full moon at the Masons Arms, Bury New Road, Whitefield. The initiation fee was £4.10.0d and subscriptions were two shillings per meeting - a far cry from the days when Ben, Tommy and their parents dined off threepence.

Ben enjoyed his new-found gentility. "I was a country gentleman for a time, walking out with my dog on an evening, and chatting with old people by the way. This dog was called 'Fly', and was a remarkable animal. She could distinguish the sound of the door bell from that of any other; and whenever I had occasion to go to the post office, nearly a mile distant, she would paw at my door when I was ready to start, to accompany me. I have often wondered how she knew the time." The dog also learnt the way to the Church Inn, "where on an evening a 'gradely sort' of company met, and whose friendship in after life became, as it were, a part of my being," and would wait under the seat for Ben to go home. Unfortunately, she wasn't clever enough to conceal her knowledge when the parson returned, and on Ben's next visit his friend started chuckling: "'Mister Brierley,' he said at last, 'I think you taught 'Fly' bad

A young Ben, sans beard, or as he put it "sans owt"! Undated, but this must be an early photograph, even as far as photography goes

manners while you were here.'" Ben enquired why he thought this. "'Well,' he replied, good humourdly, 'I went the other day to the post-office, and when I had posted my letters 'Fly' trotted over to the 'Church Inn'. I think she must have been there before.'" Ben was forced to own up!

"Ab o'th'Yate", as pictured in Ben Brierley's Journal

On their return from Stand, the Brierleys settled down once again to life in Collyhurst and as a result Ben signed a petition to form the Masonic Wilton Lodge, named in honour of the Earls of Wilton who occupied Heaton House until the estate was purchased by Manchester Corporation early this century; it is now the largest public park in the city.

The letter which accompanied the petition gives a flavour of the times. "Blackley is a village distant three to four miles from Manchester and numbered at the last census 4,112 souls; there is, however, in addition, the villages of Crumpsall, Harpurhey and Moston, all within a radius of two miles and comprising a population altogether of about 14,000, for which there is no Masonic convenience.

The nearest Lodge to the one contemplated is the 'Imperial George', Middleton, distant from two to three miles between which there is neither Railway nor other

Public conveyance. I may state that through Crumpsall, Harpurhey and Blackley there is no Railway communication, nor is there any public conveyance with the first named and the city, with the two latter. However, Omnibuses run occasionally, the last of which leave Blackley at 7.5 for the city, hence after their Masonic duties are ended, the Brethren are under the necessity of engaging private conveyances, or otherwise reach their homes at unreasonable hours."

Ben Brierley never held office in the Wilton Lodge. He was probably too busy, for about this time he wrote his third serial story, "My Grandmother's Clockcase". He later lamented that it had never appeared in book form, "I know not why." It was this tale in which "Ab o'th'Yate", the quaint nom de plume under which Ben was to publish some of his best work, put in his first appearance.

Ab o'th'Yate

The character who first appeared in "My Grandmother's Clockcase" and was introduced to a wider circle in "Ab o'th'Yate on Times and Things" became really famous with Ben's "Ab o'th'Yate in London", the most successful of all his works up to that point. Ben wrote of his alter ego in later life: "In all that I have written I have striven to rescue the Lancashire character from the erroneous conceptions of 'Tim Bobbin.' The Lancashire man is not necessarily a representative of clownishness. In matters where sound common sense is required he is capable of holding his own with the natives of any other county."

'Tim Bobbin' was, of course, the Lancashire dialect writer John Collier (died 1786) and Ben's comment is neither entirely fair to him, nor entirely consistent. Jean and Peter Bond point out in "Tim Bobbin Lives!" (1986), that Ben wrote a poem for a memorial service held beside Tim Bobbin's grave in Rochdale Churchyard in 1892. In it he hailed Tim as "Cervantes, Hogarth, rolled in one!" This is, as the Bonds say, "a bit overblown. Tim was certainly not Cervantes. (Unlike Don Quixote's windmills, Tim's adversaries were real enough.) Neither was he Hogarth. But he was a man of many talents and an unforgettable character."

Perhaps the same could be said of Ben himself. He certainly believed in his characters: "I have not marshalled a lot of dummies before the public. There is not one that is upholstered - not one in whose composition the presence of the least stuffing can be detected. They are men and women as I have known them in life - never been set up for angels, nor degraded by being posed as bigger fools than can be found elsewhere. These I leave as my legacy to my native county; it is the only one I can leave; and if conscientiousness be any recommendation, it may be accepted with every trust."

Ab, or to give him his Sunday name, "Abraham of the Gate", was, like Ben's other characters, based on reality. Proper names mattered not in the days when folk were described by where their homes were or how they earned their living (hence Sal Upsteps, Mally at th'raintub, Pie Sally), but Ben did give his character a surname and "Abraham Fletcher" supposedly dwelt in "Walmsley Fowt", along with his good wife Sal and their children Joe and Betty, Dick and young Ab. (Ben seemed to invent new children to suit a story-line.) He was called "Ab o'th'Yate" because his cottage stood by the gate leading into Walmsley Fold. In real life "Walmsley Fowt" was Bardsley Fold and Ab was based on the equally real Job Ogden, who lived there. A massive photograph of the cottage and gate which is said to have given rise to the idea hangs in Failsworth Public Library with John Moore, landlord

Bardsley Fold, the original of "Walmsley Fowt". Job Ogden's cottage is on the right

of the Bridge Inn, standing guard. The photograph must have been taken in the early 1880s as it was included in the album presented to Ben on his second trip to America (see page 35). Incidentally, the word "gate" didn't refer originally to the wooden structure hanging between two posts, but rather to the opening itself, or "get" through them.

The kind of thing that went on in "Walmsley Fowt" is exemplified by the following story. It was a bitter winter and a woman wanted a square of glass putting into one of her quarrels (a small pane of glass in a larger window). She employed a man who, unbeknown to her, cut a square of ice off the pond and fixed it. He was paid, and beat a hasty retreat. The woman was to be seen over the next few days standing at her front door, rolling pin in hand, looking up and down the Fold. Neighbours commented on how much baking she was doing lately. Such were Ab's tales - well-written, humorous sketches that even a child could understand.

And his audiences loved them. Although Ben came from the "industrial" end of Failsworth, he enjoyed going to the "rural" end to give readings of his works, for there was emerging a new type of person at this time, one who could read and write but still lived in the area where they had been born and brought up. These people understood writers such as Ben Brierley and they recognised themselves and their neighbours in the stories. They could identify. I suppose it was like the "Coronation Street" of the day; most people enjoyed it and wanted more. Ben provided more.

The Manchester Literary Club started a weekly publication entitled "Country Words", edited by Charles Hardwick, and in this appeared Ben's "Epistle to Edwin Waugh" and "The Marlocks of Merriton". The variation in spelling of "Merriton" in different editions of the work is most entertaining - it was Ben's pet name for Middleton, of course, and is shown on no known map. So we get the likes of "Meriton", "Merridon" and I even own an 1884 copy where "Merritan" on the spine has been overstamped by the correct version. Ben did well to get the whole lot into "Country Words", for the journal lasted only seventeen weeks! This was a busy time for him, however, and he was writing sketches for all kinds of publications: "To eleven weekly papers I contributed week by week instalments of my best known work, with the exception of 'Daisy Nook', 'Ab o'th'Yate in London.'"

After Ab himself, perhaps Ben's most used character was "Fause Juddie", or if you want a translation, "Knowing George". "George Taylor" was the fiddling (with a bow or otherwise) badger, or shopkeeper, whom Ab used to tease constantly. James Middleton, writing in the 1920s, claimed to know the identity of the model for Fause Juddie and said that it was not the Dob Lane shopkeeper named John Taylor, as many people thought, but another who lived higher up and on the opposite side of the road. "His true name was Wright, but his common name was 'Reet'. He kept a mixed business and 'sowd ale'. As to this changing of names, there used to be a man called Wright Wright, who was commonly referred to as Wright Reet. Perhaps this was a reproof to his parents for their inconsiderateness on christening day." I hope that makes the matter crystal clear!

Actually it isn't as clear as all that, for in Ben's "Marlocks of Merriton" the schoolmaster is a certain "Fause Juddie", and I don't think they are meant to be the same person. In the issue of Ben

"Item"

Also; a word used when any article is added to the former. Owd Bowser used to fuddle a week at once at th' "Gowden Bo;" but he'd never a haupenny in his pocket at th' time. If he coed for a fresh pint, he'd ha' said "Tell Bill." That meant "set it on." His wife would ha' gone th' week after, an' ha' paid th' shot. But ther a new londlort ut coome fro' Manchester, an' i'stead o' chalkin ale scores up at back o' th' kitchen dur, he wrote 'em in a book. Bowser didno' like that, becose he couldno' see heaw he're gooin on. One day he'd a bit of a dust wi' th' londlort, becose he thowt he're reckonin too mich. "There's *item* so-an'-so," Mesther Bunghole kept sayin. "*Item* be-*dashed*," Bowser broke eaut at last; "I never tasted a drop o' *item* i' my life. I shall pay for nowt nobbut fourpenny." They'n coed th' londlort "Little Item" ever sin'

From "Ab o'th'Yate's Dictionary"

Brierley's Journal for December 26th 1885, Ben wrote Juddie's obituary, mentioning that he was seventy-five when he died. I wonder why he bumped off one of his most useful characters? Perhaps the real Juddie had passed away and he didn't want to mock the dead.

One of Ben's models, however, did own up - it was said that Samuel Broadbent of Mossley, once involved in the silk trade of Woodhouses, was proud to be the origin of "Sam Smithies" of "Eatin' a Bootjack" fame. But the true identity of the workshy "Billy Softly" was never revealed - Ben could be discreet when necessary. Whether it was innate kindliness or fear of retribution that prompted the discretion in this case, we shall never know!

Samuel Laycock and Edwin Waugh

Oldham has its Ben Brierley Way, but Failsworth has to make do with Brierley Avenue, situated in the "Poets' Corner" along with Waugh Avenue and Laycock Grove and Crescent. (Brierley, Waugh and Laycock are often

Samuel Laycock

Sim Schofield

referred to as the "Trinity" in Lancashire dialect writing.)

Sam Laycock was born in Marsden, West Yorkshire, in 1826 but moved over to "us" in his formative years. He wrote in the East Lancashire dialect of the time, and very good he was too! Perhaps his most famous work is "Bonny Brid", written in the mid-1800s in anticipation of a son being born, but when Hannah presented herself to the world, he refused to change the words (perhaps he couldn't find a rhyme for "lass"). In later years Hannah married Sim Schofield, author of "Short Stories about Failsworth Folk", published in 1905 and reissued the following year (still containing all the glaring errors from the first edition, especially in the chapter concerning our mutual friend Ben Brierley). Sim and Hannah lived at Auburn Bank, New Moston, Failsworth, for a time. The terrace of three still stands and I can see it out of my window as I write.

For health reasons, Sam Laycock moved to Fleetwood and then to Blackpool in his later years and, amongst other things, took up the then new art of photography; in fact I possess a rare sepia print bearing the legend "Sam Laycock, Photographer, Blackpool" of Ben's only child, Annie, who died of tuberculosis ("the poor man's disease").

Let's hear from Ben at last. His acquaintance with Sam began late in life and, like most of us, he had formed a mental image of the man he was to meet before the introduction. How wrong we can be! Ben wrote, "I had pictured him in my mind as being a robust, rollicking fellow. Instead of that I found him to be nearly all head, his body being only attached to it as a kind of support." Ben got to know him better after he left Fleetwood and often sat for him in his Blackpool studio.

"I remember him on one occasion getting his temper into a white heat as I sat waiting for the camera to fire at me. Sam was rubbing his glass with a wash-leather at the time, and the harder he rubbed the friction on his mind seemed to keep company." The cause of the annoyance was that someone had been pirating one of Sam's poems and he was planning to take the miscreant to court (he later did so successfully and got five pounds damages). In an attempt to placate him, Ben said, "Sam, how is it nobody offers to steal anything of mine?"
"Your name's not Laycock," was the reply.
"Oh, I see."

They met again the following October and Sam asked Ben whether he got many engagements to give readings. Ben replied, "As many as I care to fulfil."
"Strange! I get none," he remarked.

Edwin Waugh

"Your name's not Brierley," said Ben.

"Sam saw the point at once and his face opened out into a grotesque grin, the prelude to a hearty laugh."

Game, set and match!

Ben's friendship with Edwin Waugh, born at Rochdale in 1817, went back much further and for a time in the 1860s they were in almost nightly companionship, when their engagements allowed. Together with several friends, they formed the habit of meeting at the Clarence or the nearby Shakespeare in Manchester or the Balmoral, Rochdale Road, behind which Ben lived at the time. Sim Schofield tells a story of when they had been giving readings together to a particularly unresponsive audience at Blackpool. They had made barely enough money to cover the cost of hiring the hall and had to walk back to their lodgings in a heavy downpour. A dog, half-drowned, its tail between its legs, scuttled past them. "'Does theaw see that dog?' Waugh said to Brierley. 'Aye, aw do,' replied Ben. 'Well, it strikes me,' Waugh continued, 'that dog's bin givin' readin's.'"

To Annie Brierley's eleventh birthday party her parents invited eleven of her schoolmates and one other guest, Edwin Waugh. Ben and his wife were getting supper, when suddenly, "I heard a loud yell of delight proceeding from the parlour. Eager to ascertain what was the cause of all this fun, I entered the room. There was a sight for a student in natural history - Waugh on all-fours, pacing round the room with two children on his back, 'doing the Belle Vue elephant,' and now and then giving a roar, after the well known *pachyderm* who carries all sizes and ages of children round the 'course' at the zoological gardens in Hyde Road." (As this was written many years after the event, Ben was probably thinking of Maharajah, the elephant which was brought to Belle Vue in 1872.)

Things hadn't always been so amicable. Ben had composed a parody on Waugh's "Come Whoam to thi Childer an' Me" entitled "Go Tak thi Ragged Childer an' Flit", describing his friend as a "Great dhrunken slotch". Ben's version was printed and published by Abel Heywood & Son and sold many thousands of copies, and Waugh was not amused! A coolness ensued, made worse by the fact that, through a misunderstanding, they found themselves in competition for the same job. If he saw Ben approaching, Waugh would cross the road, or dart into a shop or otherwise snub him. This upset Ben very much, to the extent that he could hardly eat or sleep, and Esther became very worried about the state of affairs. Ben composed a long poem headed "The Two Robins" (it contained twenty verses even after shortening), trying to lure Waugh back into his friendship. The original version began by depicting the grief borne by poor robin Ben at being forsaken by his brother robin Ned. It was shortened by three or four verses and the title changed to "To Edwin Waugh", and then published in "Country Words" (1866-7) and the supplementary portion of the "Manchester Weekly News", or as the snubbers called it, "Manchester Weakly News". It worked!

The story of their reconciliation was told to James Dronsfield by a man named Thomas Lythgoe, who was staying with Ben and Esther at the time. Lythgoe and Ben were on Rochdale Road the Monday after publication and as they reached the bridge nearly opposite Reather Street, Waugh loomed up. "Ben, forgie me!" (Note: Waugh apologised, and not Ben.) "O reet, lad." It was an emotional moment. "The two stood looking at each other as well as they could, for tears of joy by the one, and of regret by the other, were streaming down their cheeks." To cut a long story short, they went to celebrate the reunion in the Old Fox Hotel, Victoria Street. Lythgoe left early, but "It was not until very late that [Ben] landed," and he had to be assisted to a chair. I know the feeling, and I sympathise!

"Intrusion"

Gooin into company wheere yo'r noane wanted.

From "Ab o'th'Yate's Dictionary"

Ben Brierley's Journal

Let's leave Ben sleeping it off in his chair, perhaps dreaming of the day he would be able to edit his own publication. He achieved his aim in the April of 1869, when Ben Brierley's Journal saw the light of day. It started life as a monthly, costing twopence and was largely self-penned, having the sub-title "Journal of Literature, Science, and Art, for the Promotion of Good-will and Good-fellowship among men". Issue No.5 (August) sold 13,000 copies, "Without employing street boys to push it under the noses of the public". So this issue alone raked him in well over £100. Of course, he had to lay out for paper, printing, wages and so on, but it was still slightly better than the 3d he had received for hauling coals from Limeside Pits!

The Journal was well established by 1874, when Ben's brother-in-law, James Firth, who had been working in London as an advertising manager, fell ill and wanted to come home. Ben saw how useful he could be, so they went into partnership as "Brierley & Firth, publishers" and took offices on Deansgate. Ben Brierley's Journal became a weekly, put out every Saturday and costing a penny.

"Business was progressing satisfactorily," Ben wrote, "when the greatest calamity of my life befel me; I lost my only child." The day before her death, the following notice appeared in the Journal: "Years of unremitting hard work, and a long period of distressing anxiety caused by severe and protracted illness in the family, necessitate that our Mr Brierley should take a season of comparative rest." Humorous writing (as in his "Ab o'th'Yate Sketches") was out of the question for some time and the circulation of the Journal went down. "My partner's health continued to decline, and we agreed to give up the business." The last issue to appear under the banner of Brierley & Firth was that for 28th August 1875. By September they had sold the Journal to Abel Heywood & Son, who were still publishing it in 1891.

Abel Heywood was quite a character in his own right. Born in Prestwich in 1810, as a young man he found himself helping to support his widowed mother on a wage of one shilling and sixpence a week. Thrown out of work when he was twenty, he became an agent for the sale of a political paper called "The Poor Man's Guardian", which was published in London. At that time there was a government tax on newspapers called stamp duty, which was vigorously opposed by Radicals as a tax on knowledge. "The Poor Man's Guardian" bore no government stamp and in March 1832 Abel Heywood was summoned before a magistrate called Mr Foster and fined fifty-four pounds for breaking the Stamp Laws. He refused to pay the fine and spent four months in the New Bailey Prison. "The Poor Man's Guardian" became an important element in the campaign against stamp duty and after a court had declared it was not an illegal newspaper, the duty was reduced to a penny in 1836; it was finally abolished in 1855.

Having been on the receiving end of the law, Abel must have been quite delighted to be appointed a Commissioner of Police in 1836. He was elected councillor in 1843, became an alderman ten years later and was twice Mayor of Manchester, in fact he became known as the "Father of Manchester Corporation". He was chairman of the Town Hall Committee when the present Manchester Town Hall was built in the 1870s, and the hour bell in use today is known as "Big Abel" after him. It bears his initials, "AH", and a line from Tennyson, "Ring out the false, ring in the true." It weighs eight tons, two hundredweight and was installed in 1882 to replace the original hour bell, which was claimed to be the second largest perfect clock bell in England. (Peter of York was the largest; Big Ben was larger, but cracked! Read into that what you will!)

Abel Heywood

"Temptation"

Stondin at a cookshop window after clemmin a day, an' havin nowt to spekilate with. Th' *temptation's* stronger when there's a smell comes eaut o' th'kitchen. I knew a mon ut used to goo a-watchin hungry lads, an' when he seed they could abide no longer he'd give 'em thrippence apiece for a blow-eaut.

From "Ab o'th'Yate's Dictionary"

Under Heywood's management, Ben Brierley's Journal continued to prosper - after all, it still bore Ben's name over the door, and his name could sell! It seems that Ben remained the editor and he was clearly a busy man. From February 1880 this dire warning appeared: "NOTICE: Contributions intended for insertion in 'Ben Brierley's Journal' should be accompanied by stamps for return. The Editor does not otherwise undertake to return rejected articles." Five years later he was even more irritable: "The editor wishes it to be understood that the office of the Journal is at 56 & 58 Oldham Street, Manchester, and NOT at his residence." Perhaps he was heartily sick of being bombarded by "piffle". I do hope he hadn't become smug!

But his criticisms are generally tempered with humour. Ben summed up some potential scribes in his "Ab o'th'Yate's Dictionary" ("Walmsley Fowt Skoomester") of 1881, in which he goes through the alphabet giving witty meanings to hundreds of words; it, too, was first published in the "Journal" and the definition of POET appeared in November 1880: "What every lad an' wench ut con write their name aims at bein, an' if they con put two lines t'gether wi' a jinglin' seaund, they thinken they owt to goo i' print an' be paid for, even if it's th'arrantest balderdash ut ever a lad wur threshed for. This is an average bit -

Oh, Mary are you comin out
When you hear me rap upon the spout
Or at the gate thy name to call
Or rub a brick against the wall."

VERSE gets a similar treatment: "Generally understood to be a piece o' poetry, but applied as weel to th'owd Book, tho' why I dunno' know. I' any other piece o' print it would be coed a paragraph. Verses used to be made abeaut folk when they'rn hanged, an' nice samples o' poetry they wur. This is abeaut the style:-

Come all ye youths and maidens fair,
A warning take by me,
Who must to-morrow morn be hung
Upon the gallows tree.

It is for murdering Nancy Brown;
Oh, shameful to relate,
I cut her throat from ear to ear,
Which brings me to this fate.

What are Solomon's songs, compared to that?"

Annie Brierley, photographed about 1870

To Death

O DEATH! thou art no fiend, when to thy arms
Thou takest the weary pilgrim of despair;
Thou art not terrible when thou dost seize
On him, who hath outlived his happiness.
The man of sorrow hails thee as his friend;-
Thou dost not smite him; in thy close embrace
He struggles not; but yearns with strong desire
To lift the awful veil, which shrouds thy form,
And gaze upon thy placid loveliness.
To him thy face is circled round with smiles,
Which to a soul unwean'd of earth are hid;
But shine on sorrow with alluring ray,
And tempt the life-sick wanderer to the tomb.

Yet, thou seem'st cruel, Death! when thou dost pluck
The bud of childhood ripening into youth,
Crushing the germ of beauty fresh from heaven,
And pois'ning with sepulchral taint its life.
Dost thou, stern reaper! gather them in pride
To decorate thy subterranean bower?
Or, to entwine around thy diadem,
As we would deck with Flora's progeny
The garland of a bride?
O! let us hope,
That thou dost cull them with a loving hand,
To plant them in a more salubrious clime-
Twining their tendrils 'round the throne of God,
That they may bloom and ripen 'neath His smile.

Annie Brierley, and Ben's Life in Politics

Back to 1875 and the loss of Ben and Esther's only child, Annie. She died of general tuberculosis on Sunday 13th June at 12 St Oswald's Grove, Collyhurst, and the death was certified by John Armstrong MRCS, LM, LSA, of Park House, 767 Rochdale Road.

Annie had been looking forward to acting as a bridesmaid at a cousin's wedding and begged her mother that she could wear the new dress she had selected for the occasion, even if she wasn't well enough to attend the ceremony. The wish was granted. Ben's friend, the author Charles Hardwick wrote, "She was suffering. A doubt would have been cruel, and it was not whispered. The bridesmaid was ready! Dressed in the beautiful wedding raiment prepared for her, and arranged in all the dainty garniture becoming such a day of gladness, the beautiful girl was ready - as she lay white and dead in her coffin."

Charles Hardwick continued, "The story was so strange and pitiful that all the country side was saddened by it. Kind-hearted neighbours and pitying crowds mournfully pressed for leave to look upon a sight so fair and sad; and from long distances they came and came, and were not denied. And thus Ben's one ewe lamb, the little princess, lay in her coffin beautiful and in State, like a Pontiff or an Emperor, her eyes closed softly in a dream of happiness, and her pale lips, on which a faint smile lay like a flower, sealed with an everlasting silence! The scene will not be soon effaced from the memory of many a sobbing, pitying beholder."

Ben's autobiography attributes this quotation to Charles Hadfield, but the Journal indexes consistently name Charles Hardwick. It was a natural mistake to make. Both men were friends, both had written for the Journal and Hadfield died in June 1884, when Ben was working on "Home Memories", and would have been uppermost in his mind. Charles Hadfield was born in Glossop, but came to Manchester very young and attended the Mechanics Institute in Cooper Street. He trained as a house painter, but after winning prizes for essays he became a journalist and at various times edited the Manchester City News, the Warrington Examiner and the Salford Weekly News. His

Charles Hardwick

obituary appeared in Ben Brierley's Journal of 14th June 1884. Five years later, in July 1889, Ben lost another friend. Born in Preston in 1817, Charles Hardwick served his time as a printer at the Preston Chronicle, then became a portrait painter. In 1841 he joined the Oddfellows and rose to high office, becoming Grand Master of the Manchester Unity about the time he moved to Manchester in the 1850s. He had already written a history of Preston and, as mentioned earlier, was one of the founders of the Manchester Literary Club in 1862. At the same time he was editing and writing for the Oddfellows Magazine, a worthy successor to John Bolton Rogerson, who had encouraged writers like Elijah Ridings, John Critchley Prince and Ben himself. In 1846, ten years before Annie was born, Rogerson published Ben's poem, "To Death", reproduced on page 24. If Ben remembered it on the day of her funeral, it must have seemed a terrible prophecy.

Annie was buried, still wearing the bridesmaid's dress, in Harpurhey General Cemetery, in a grave that her grieving parents vowed would never be disturbed. I often wondered how they managed to achieve this while joining her under the same stone until it

In Memoriam

Annie,

Only child of Ben. and Esther Brierley;
Born November 7th, 1856. Died June 13th, 1875.

We thought she was our own for yet awhile;
That we had earn'd her, by our love of Heav'n,
To be a life's comfort, not a season's smile,
Then tears for ever. "Tis to be forgiven,"
We deemed her mortal - not an angel sent
From out a mission host, on mercy bent.

We were beguiled by her sweet ways of love-
The growth of her affections round two stems-
As if they were of her, and from above,
We did not note that from her heart the gems
Of her devotion were bestrewn in show'rs
Where'er she went, and gathered like spring flowers.

And her last words (coherent) - "I have lived,
And have not lived" - were full of earthly tone
And utterance. They, too, our hearts deceived;
Nor were we mindful till, when left alone,
We heard the flutter of a dove-like wing,
And a sweet strain, such as the seraphs sing.

Then knew we she had come in mortal guise,
To teach us love, and charity, and grace;
With sun-gold in her hair, heaven in her eyes,
And all that's holy in her preaching face.
The scales had fallen, and our vision then
Saw that an angel graced the homes of men.

dawned on me that it was a double plot: Annie lies in 3259 and Ben and Esther in 3260. The present-day stone over the Brierleys' grave was erected after Ben's death in 1896. Poor Annie did have a stone before this, but it was kindly removed to make way for Ben's more impressive monolith. There is a flat stone in front of the "new" monument and I'd like to turn it over and see if it holds any writing, but I don't think I will.

Ben's memorial stone says of her,

"It came up late in the
Spring, and bloomed
at harvest Time, the
reaper wept as he
gathered the shorn
flower and bound it,
with the ripened grain,
in the sheaf of the
eternal. B.B."

It does help if your father is a poet! The original stone held another verse as well:

We thought she was our own for yet awhile;
That we had earned her, by our love of Heaven,
To be a life's comfort, not a season's smile,
Then tears for ever.

Within eighteen months of Annie's death her uncle, James Firth, had gone too and his grave is the next plot along. His rather ordinary, upright slab informs the reader that he died in London and there is an inscription which runs,

We'll mourn with still regret,
As for a star in daylight lost,
But not in darkness set.

Ben was advised to get himself back into public life as a distraction from his melancholy, and this he did by standing as a Liberal candidate for St Michael's Ward in the local elections. Although his candidature was almost regarded as a joke - some people thinking that it was Ab o'th'Yate hissel' putting up - he was not long in proving to his constituents that their confidence had not been misplaced. In November 1875 Ben got 2,817 votes, Mr R T Walker 2,628 votes.

St Michael's Ward was named after St Michael's Church that stood at the bottom of Angel Street, off Rochdale Road, a very poor district of the time. Charles Hardwick summed it up a few years later: "It is hard to realise the magnitude of it. When I am told by Ben Brierley - who ought to know, for he sat for [6] years as its representative in the City Council - that you can carve out of this multitudinous aggregation of human beings 12,000 householders and call it St Michael's Ward, you begin to feel helpless in the presence of a fact which Mr Richard Swiveller would call a 'staggerer'." Twenty polling booths were set up in St Oswald's Church Schools to accommodate them, but many of the voters were illiterate and for one man at least the outcome was not as he had intended. He vowed he would rather slit his throat than vote for Mr Walker and promptly put a large cross in the box opposite Walker's name, thinking that this would "cross him out"! Another lady asked how much it cost after she had voted. Out of this "multitudinous aggregation" of people only 5,445 votes were cast in the case of Brierley v Walker. Education was badly needed and some people voted for Ben on the grounds that he was "the educator of the people". No doubt the Manchester Guardian, a liberal newspaper, intended to pay the Liberal candidate a compliment when they summed up the situation, but it didn't quite come out right: "The number of illiterates in this ward was very large, and it was remarked that a very large majority of them supported Mr Brierley."

Ben in his City Councillor's robes. It did not make him pompous, for he described his début as follows: "For the first time I strutted forth, arrayed in my apportionment of civic purple." ("A Flourish of Trumpets", 1875)

One of Ben's first official engagements was recorded by James Middleton. It was the unveiling of the statue of Oliver Cromwell, which was presented to Manchester by Abel Heywood's wife in memory of her first husband, Alderman Goadsby. Middleton writes, "There was a municipal procession, the first I had ever seen. It was a terribly wet day, and the city fathers could only be imperfectly recognised under dripping umbrellas. I remember seeing the erect figure of Ben Brierley, the one man whom I could identify."

James, a friend and admirer of Ben Brierley, was born at Newton Heath in 1853. As well as running a grocery business in Hollinwood, he was a public speaker and freelance journalist. He was elected to Oldham Town Council for Hollinwood Ward in 1897 and was Mayor of Oldham in 1916-17, but he is probably best known for writing "Oldham Past and Present" in 1903 and "The Old Road" in 1920. He died on 13th October 1925 and was laid to rest in St Margaret's Churchyard, Hollinwood (my mother attended the funeral).

Ben would have attended the old Town Hall on the corner of Cross Street and King Street, but the new Town Hall was already under construction and the council first met in the new building in February 1877. The formal opening took place on 13th September that year and the Mayor, Alderman Heywood, led the city council in procession from the old Town Hall to the new. Guards of honour from both cavalry and infantry were in attendance, and delegations from Manchester Fire Brigade and the City Police joined the parade. I don't know what they expected to find when they got there, as the Waterworks Department had been in residence since July 1875! The columns from the old Town Hall stand in Heaton Park, on the opposite side of the lake to the old Lakeside Café, where Ben's stone tribute is crumbling also. It's a small world.

Ben's maiden speech, on 3rd May 1876, was in support of the Free Libraries Committee. Someone had suggested moving the Reference Library to the "attic" of the new Town Hall, and the Committee was naturally much against the idea. Ben, too, felt that to place the collection out of reach of the public for whom it was intended would be legislating backwards, "unless it was the desire of the Corporation to preserve the library in the same way that the old women did their copper kettles - never allowing them to be used. - (Hear, hear.)" He pointed out that there had been no objections a few months earlier, when the Watch Committee had asked for £40,000 to enlarge its "palatial residence" for the criminal population, but when the Libraries Committee asked "that a powerful instrument in preventing crime might be properly and not extravagantly housed, they were told that the attic in the Town Hall was quite good enough for the purpose." Commenting that a reference library you couldn't get at was of little use, he went on, "Locating it at an altitude that could not be reached without having to climb steps to the number of 120, would be like placing a bit of bread on a dog's nose and counting 120 before allowing it to be snapped up." (Loud laughter.) Having got his audience going, Ben warmed to his subject and began to elaborate on the expedition "to explore the mysterious regions of the carillons", concluding that "none but such adventurous spirits as the Mayor and Mr Alderman Heywood would ever have the hardihood to climb that giddy height." He had gone up with a party who had set out all at once, but "like amateur mountaineers climbing Ben Lomond," had gradually become separated, "some hanging on here and there by a balustrade, and others trying to emulate the pranks of their boyish days by a grotesque attempt to look nimble." (Laughter.) "By dint of dogged perseverance they all reached the top, but not in a body. They turned up in panting and perspiring driblets," (Laughter), "the last man being a little over ten minutes behind his immediate predecessor." (Renewed laughter.) If the ascent was so difficult for the "active and energetic" members of the City Council, Ben asked wickedly, what would it be

Those Town Hall Stairs

After Long- Short-or-any-other-fellow

The shades of night were falling fast,
As up the Town Hall steps there passed,
A man who on his shoulders bore
Full seventy winters, - and he swore -
"These cursed stairs!"

Firmly he grasped an alpen-stock,
To help his legs from block to block;
And as he toiled his way along,
Throughout each corridor there rang -
"Confound these stairs!"

From warehouse window came no light,
Which could illume that misty height;
And when he found himself alone,
From out his breast escaped a groan -
"These Town Hall stairs!"

"Whither go'st thou?" a porter said,
With buttons on his coat o'erspread.
"I go to con historic lore;
But clamber up, I'll never more,
These Town Hall stairs."

A maiden old, with features brown,
The balusters was cleaning down;
And as the pilgrim raised his head,
Half-frightened at the sight, she said -
"Oh, drat these stairs!"

Rough was the night, the storm without,
A torrent made in lead and spout,
And rattled 'gainst the window pane,
That none could hear the echo, vain -
"Where are the stairs?"

At early morn, as duty-ward
The porters trod the pavement hard,
They heard a voice call from on high,
As if 'twere shouted from the sky, -
"Where are the stairs?"

There, on the cold Mosaic, lay
An old man, bent, and worn, and grey.
He'd been locked in; and as he grasped
An alpen-stock, he faintly gasped-
"These Town Hall stairs."

Ye who of Helicon have quaffed,
And studied till you're nearly daft,-
Is this the watchword of your craft,
You'd shout along the spiral shaft-
"Excelsior?"

Oh, what would Grundy say, or Lamb,
If, without aid of 'bus, or tram,
They'd thus to climb, their heads to cram?
"All right, 'Excelsior,' but d---
These Town Hall stairs!"

like for "men of more than ordinary bulk and when getting into years"? He followed this up by reading a humorous poem he had written for the occasion, a parody on Longfellow's "Excelsior" entitled "Those Town Hall Stairs" (reproduced on page 27) and sat down among shouts of laughter and cheers.

The resolution in favour of housing the library properly was carried by a large majority and the chairman of the Libraries Committee, Alderman Baker, congratulated Ben, saying, "No other man on the council could have done it!" In the event, the library was housed in the old Town Hall until 1912. Thus a self-educated weaver, not so many years away from the loom, had championed the cause of learning in Manchester, a service that has not yet been acknowledged.

Dizzy heights: a view looking north-east from the top of the new Town Hall. The dome of the Infirmary at Piccadilly can be seen under the statue's hand. Fountain Street, where Ben worked for a time, crosses the centre of the picture beneath the statue

Ben's municipal experiences, especially in connection with the Nuisances Committee, led him to raise the question, "What shall we do with our poor?" No man was better qualified to give an opinion on the subject, and he served on a greater number of committees and sub-committees than perhaps any other member of the Corporation: Nuisances; Hackney Coach; Lamp and Scavenging; Parks and Cemeteries, and Baths and Wash-houses. He was a great believer in self-help and in the beneficial effects of nature, and as such a keen supporter of those who organised flower shows in an effort to give city dwellers an interest which might brighten their lives: "A man with a flower in his coat looks upwards; and you may depend upon it that in nine cases out of ten that flower will be matched by a clean shirt front... The lovers of flowers fill not our gaols, nor are they to be found loitering about gin-shop doors."

This wasn't just pious Victorian morality; Ben was well aware of the problems of what would now be called the inner city, and his practical charity is reflected in "A Ragged Rant", in which he describes a seaside trip (of which he was an eye witness and, no doubt, an active supporter) arranged by Wood Street Mission for the poor boys and girls of Manchester and Salford. "The Manchester & Salford Street Children's Mission" started life in 1869 in Lombard Street, moving to its more famous address in 1873, when the railway company acquired the Lombard Street land for building Central Station. Alfred Alsop, the founder, assisted by a handful of friends, scoured the neighbourhood of Deansgate, "a very hot-bed of social iniquity and vice", for children sleeping out on the street, or in doorways, and took them into care. Many boys were found regular employment, and quite a few were helped to emigrate to Canada and America. No doubt some of these "ragged ranters" paid their cents in the 1880s to listen to Ben Brierley when he visited the States. Mr Alsop died in 1892 at the early age of forty-seven, but the work of Wood Street Mission continues; their modus operandi may have changed, but their aim has not. Back in 1879 the discipline was strict, as Ben recalled with some amusement: "The simultaneous immersion of 250 boys in the receding tide was a sight not to be forgotten. The bathers were formed in line; and at the word - 'Turn cartwheel, and into the water,' the scene can be better imagined than described. We have only to fancy the flinging up of 500 bare legs at one time, to realise a picture that must have been exceedingly picturesque."

Ben Brierley as "The Lancashire Weaver Lad" - a sketch once owned by his friend, Samuel Gradwell

He was a keen observer, and his gentle humour was never far from the surface. Manchester's town clerk for many years was the formidable Sir Joseph Heron, noted for his ability to get things done and for the care he took with his appearance. When the magnificent new Town Hall was built, Ben - no doubt remembering the stairs - suggested that the building be named "The Heronry". No one else would have dared!

But humour went hand in hand with hard work and in the winter of 1878 Ben assisted in no fewer than twenty-two stage entertainments for various relief organisations, always giving his services free and paying his own expenses.

He was on stage again the following September, with his friend Robert Dottie (R Dick). They appeared together at the Theatre Royal on Peter Street, Manchester, in Ben's own drama, "The Lancashire Weaver Lad". James Middleton, in his 1920 publication "The Old Road", recalled another Failsworth character who had a hand in the production. His name was "Owd Crink", and he was the regular trainer of the morris dancers in the Failsworth district, going every year to the Bell (now the Blue Bell) in Moston for that purpose. He was engaged to do the same thing for "The Weaver Lad", but "he had a very poor opinion of the stage company he had to train. 'He could ha' larnt a lot o' Failsworth lads i' one hauve o'th'time,' so he said to the author of the play."

Poverty persists: outside Wood Street Mission in 1900

From this play came Ben's song, "The Wayver of Welbrook", which was accompanied by the singer using exaggerated arm and leg movements to imitate a weaver at his loom.

Wi my pickers an' pins,
An' my wellers to th'shins,
My linderins, shuttle, and yealdhook,
My treddles an'sticks,
My weight-ropes an'bricks, -
What a life! - said the Wayvor o' Welbrook.

Ben once rendered it to a crowd of surprised inmates - or as Robert Dottie dubbed them "The Lunys" - at their annual Christmas treat in the workhouse. Dottie recalled it as an amazing performance, with Ben seated on a chair flailing his limbs about in a most alarming manner in front of an invisible loom, crooning the above ditty all the while - until one "quare lookin piece o' humanity" came up to him and, looking him straight in the eye, said, "Aw say, owd lad, it'll noan be so lung afoor tha wears a Scotch cap an a corderoy suit!" (In other words, Ben would soon be joining them!)

American Visits

By the time Ben was fifty-five his health had begun to fail and in an attempt to regain it, he took his first trip to America in 1880, accompanied by Samuel Gradwell of Shudehill, to whom "Ab o'th'Yate in Yankeeland" is dedicated. They set out for Liverpool on Thursday 22nd April on the Cheshire Lines railway and would have left from the then relatively new Central Station, opened in 1877. (Readers who are not railway buffs should now prop open their eyes with matchstalks and learn that the Cheshire Lines Committee was formed by Act of Parliament on 5th July 1865, and had strong claims to be Britain's premier joint line. Although the C.L.C never owned, nor had its emblem on any locomotives, it *did* sport its own coaching stock and so many people came to see Ben off that they filled two saloon coaches.)

Arriving at Liverpool Central (opened on 2nd March 1874), they had a good feed at the Queens Hotel before boarding a boat which would take them to join the steamship City of Berlin, moored downstream. The 'City' was of the Inman Line and is recorded in the Manchester Guardian as having sailed that afternoon.

It was quite an adventure that Ben was undertaking, for the trip was not the common occurrence that it is today. The Titanic was only a dream, and we all know what happened to that! They stopped off at Queenstown, Ireland, to pick up the mails and arrived at New York on Sunday, May 2nd.

They stayed at the Metropolitan Hotel, Broadway and were introduced to lager by a distant relative of Ben's, "Will o'Jimmy's", who had come to meet them. On being asked by "Ab" what lager was, Will replied, "A sort o'ale ut doesno' mak'em drunken"! Impressed by the size of the hotels and the size of the meals, Ben didn't think much of American women, whom he considered lazy and over-indulged. He found the elaborate cemeteries places of peace and beauty, but he didn't like New York, where "the abominable stink given out by one of America's greatest sources of wealth, petroleum, pervades everywhere." The "Elevated Railroad" came in for some testy criticism, for "Ab" got a hot cinder stuck between his collar and his neck. The peevish tone in which Ben wrote, "These elevated railroads are a great nuisance in many ways, and not likely to be adopted in England," leads me to suspect that this incident was not entirely fictional!

From there he went to Paterson, New Jersey, back to New York again and on to Canada, where he stayed at the Queen's Hotel, Toronto, on 16th May. He was dragged reluctantly to visit Niagara, which from a distance he thought "a gradely Yankee sell" and no more wonderful than "an owd silver gridiron". But when

Sam Gradwell and his hotel on Shudehill (right)

he got near, it was a different story. What looked to him at first like millions of loads of hay being tumbled over a rock suddenly changed into "mountains stricken wi' th' rod o'Moses, an' melted down, an' tryin to find another resting place... Like th' shifting slides of a magic lantern it grew into another an' moore awful seet... Th' wo'ld I'd lived in had vanished; an' in that awful sound that rang, an' kept ringin', an' wur to me a summons to Judgement, I could yer angels' trumpets; an' th' singin o' thoose blessed souls ut I hoped to see ere long, tho' I felt mysel an unworthy visitor. An' this image kept grooin an' grooin, - bigger an' bigger, till I felt as if I're bein lifted off my feet, an' wur soon to join that great choir that wur fillin heaven wi' this everlastin music. Then I're startled wi' a voice that had at one time bin familiar to me - 'What dost think about th' Falls now, Ab?'"

The Merchants' Exchange, Philadelphia

It must have been quite a gruelling trip, for they went on to Ottawa and Montreal, and by 28th May were at the Parker House Hotel, Boston, where they got very drunk with some Harvard students having their annual dinner. When he woke up next morning, "Ab" discovered that "what I took to be Sammy were a towel-rail, an' I'd bin axin th' towels, I dunno' know how oft, if ther any moore ice knockin about."

On 3rd June they were at the Continental Hotel, Philadelphia, two days later at Lake George, Utah, on 7th at the Chasm Hotel, Birmingham, New York State and the next day back to Paterson, where Ben gave some readings in the Opera House, for this was a *working* holiday. The expatriate Lancastrians living in the area flocked, with their first and second generation offspring, to hear their native tongue again. What they made of Ben, reading selections from his works in the measured (some would say strangulated) Lancashire dialect harking back to the days of Chaucer, was summed up neatly when the Paterson Daily Guardian's poetical review of the year referred to,

The welcome we gave to the
Lancashire Bard,
Ben Brierley, armed with his
dialect hard.

Whilst flipping through a copy of the Oldham Chronicle Free Weekly of Thursday, 25th April 1991, my eyes set upon a "Flashback" quoting an article from a Chronicle of "100 Years Ago" - that is, 1881. It read, "Mr Benjamin Buckley, a native of Oldham, died at Paterson, New Jersey, on Wednesday, at the age of 84... He was elected President of the Senate of New Jersey in 1867, and was ex-Mayor of Paterson." No doubt Ben was saddened to read this, for it was ex-Mayor Buckley who had introduced him to his audience less than twelve months previously.

The Inman Line steamship "City of Berlin", on which Ben crossed the Atlantic in 1880

In the preface to his book, "Short Stories about Failsworth Folk", Sim Schofield, who is not renowned for his accuracy, claims that Ben took with him on his first trip to America an album of photographs donated by fans and friends, which was presented to him along with a purse of gold. The album still exists and contains snaps of local places of interest taken by Squire Knott of Oldham, in which Sim himself poses casually here and there in a black cape, no doubt "to give scale". Sim's name appears high on the list of subscribers and he was secretary of the appeal fund that raised the purse of gold, but I think that he was mistaken as to the date, having written his book almost a quarter of a century after the event. Some of the photographs were certainly taken in the USA and Canada judging by the photographers' addresses printed on the back, and these must have been put in *before* the album took its trip, as all the photos fit neatly into their various places. No! The American photos were collected on the 1880 trip and mounted in the volume along with the others, and as Ben himself states, the album was taken on the second trip.

It seems that poor old Ben - he was fifty-six by now - suffered a broken "ancliff" (ankle, to you and me) in the first days of the year following his return from the States, for he mentions it in veiled ways over and over again in his Journals of the period. He seems to have been laid up for some three or four weeks.

By April he had recovered and spent a week in Ireland, writing his pieces for inclusion in the Journal from such places as Limerick, Cork and what was then Queenstown, where he landed from this side of the water aboard the Cavan. In August, he was off to Wales for a week, as Ab o'th'Yate writes to the "Yead-hitter" (his wife!) from Llandidnodo (sic), amongst other places. He returned to Walmsley Fowt, Ab's supposed dwelling place, on August 32nd!

A mature Ben, now fully bearded

The Parker House Hotel, School Street, Boston, where Ben stayed in May 1880

About this time he moved house, to 94 St Oswald's Grove. Annie had died at number 12 and I wonder whether Ben and Esther wanted to stay in the same area but not in the house which held so many painful memories for them. Charles Hardwick, in his "A Pilgrimage through Collyhurst" of 1883, remarks, "St Oswald's Church stands, if I am not mistaken, on an eminence to the left. St Oswald's Grove is almost literally over the way. If I should say that the second mansion from the high road as you face the acclivity before you, was the present dwelling-place of 'th'owd wayver o'Wellbrook,' the consequent controversy might be carried far into the coming century!" I have seen a good photograph of the long-since-gone Grove, the entrance guarded by two high stone gateposts with provision for a nightwatchman. I'd hardly describe the houses as mansions, but it is clear that Ben was quite well off by this time. The only sad feature about the photograph is that it captures the figure of an unknown young boy travelling the high road with the aid of a walking stick. Poverty and sickness cannot be locked out by the use of gates, and Ben was to become all too familiar with both before the end. But for the present he was very busy writing regular contributions to his beloved Journal and joining a group of dignitaries who set off to open new premises in Longsight occupied by the Manchester and Salford Machine Bread Factory Limited - and sited on Baker Street!

In November 1881 he lost his seat on the council to the Conservative Mr J Faulkner by a margin of only 97 votes. The Manchester Guardian commented, "This result is generally attributed to half heartedness on the part of his friends," and complained that the elections were "confoundedly tame" as a result of dismal weather combined with widespread apathy among the voters.

Ben himself was never apathetic. If he wasn't writing for the Journal, he was writing to the newspapers. On 25th March 1870 the Reverend James Fraser was consecrated Lord Bishop of Manchester and remained so until his death on 22nd October 1885. It was a time of controversy in the Church of England - about ritual, finance, education and other matters - and the Bishop was much given to preaching about the need to bring religion to the mass of the people. A sermon on truth reported in the Manchester Guardian on 23rd April 1883 contained the statement that people seemed to be attracted to churches "from any motive rather than to get possession of truth in their souls", and Ben seized on this as an excuse to publish a tirade on religious hypocrisy. His letter appeared on 1st May and was reprinted in Ben Brierley's Journal for that month under the title "Why the Masses are kept outside the Church". It begins, sarcastically, "Bishop Fraser has again been 'effervescing', as his preaching has been called by people who evidently do not wish their consciences to be disturbed in too rude a manner. 'Can no-one stop his tongue?' asks one of these rosewater religionists. 'He is talking about everything and everybody. He condemns bazaars, pretty preaching and making things nice all round. Now he is going in for truth - the very thing to drive people out of the church, because it is not always pleasant to listen to it. What will be his next fad, I wonder? Honesty, perhaps!'"

There was much more in the same vein, including some choice examples of "Christians" who put the masses off: the tradesman who said, "It is pity that lying is a sin, it is so useful in business"; the pastor "whose failings were known to be in excess of his virtues"; the fine lady who had not paid for the dress she wore; the man whose language "savours more of Billingsgate than the shores of Galilee"; the sect who say, "If we cannot have our own way we will leave you and build a chapel in opposition to yours". Condone or condemn, Ben certainly said what he thought!

He was struggling financially now, for he had lost most of his life's savings when a building society collapsed and at the beginning of 1884 a young barrister named Tom Nash initiated a testimonial fund which was intended to send Ben to America with his pockets well lined. A dramatic performance was given at the Prince's Theatre to boost the pennies and his friends rallied round. A poem was published to celebrate the American trip, entitled "To Benjamin Brierley Esq - In view of him leaving this country for a tour of the U.S.A, wishing him God speed and a safe return". It was penned by "Arnica" of Moston Priory (the house of the Alexian

PRINCE'S THEATRE.
TUESDAY NEXT, APRIL 22.

In aid of the
BEN BRIERLEY TESTIMONIAL FUND.
And last appearance of Mr. Brierley prior to his leaving for America.

The Performances will begin at 7 30 p.m. with
Sullivan's Operatic Burlesque,
COX AND BOX.

SIGNOR SALVINI
will Recite Schiller's Poem, "THE GLOVE."

THE COBBLER'S STRATAGEM.
(A Farce by Ben Brierley.)
Solomon Makapenny, a retired grocer ....Mr. Ben Brierley.
Sam Sly, an amorous cobbler ....Mr. R. Dottie.

Twelve Dramatic Tableaux, entitled
A GAME AT CARDS,
by Chevalier-Lafosse, Mr. Warwick Brookes, and others.

The Fourth Act of Bulwer Lytton's Play,
RICHELIEU.
Richelieu.....................................Mr. J. Dewhurst.
Supported by Messrs. Charles Arnold, C. K. Shute, Louis Calvert, and James Power; and Miss Maggie Hunt, of the Claudian Company, by kind permission of Wilson Barrett, Esq.

Boxes, £1. 1s. and £2. 2s.; stalls, 6s.; circle, 5s.; upper circle, 2s. 6d.; pit, 2s.; gallery, 1s.

Advertisement for the performance at the Prince's Theatre in April 1884. In the event "A Game at Cards" was not presented; a rather huffy notice explaining that this was "in consequence of the Committee not adhering to the original Programme" appeared in the Manchester Guardian of 22nd April, signed by Augustus Lafosse of Knolls House, Higher Broughton

Bishop James Fraser

Brothers on St Mary's Road). Failsworth gave Ben a farewell soirée and Sam Laycock, unable to attend in person, also put pen to paper:

While London reared Dickens, and others as great,
It was Failsworth that reared the renowned Ab-o'th'-Yate.
It was here the weaver lad spent his young days,
And here as a man he composed his first lays;
And it seems only natural, and fitting, that now,
When age and the deep lines of care mark his brow,
You should honour the bard with his silvery hairs,
And as far as you can do so - lighten his cares...

Ben was also fêted at Manchester, Oldham, Leigh and Clayton Bridge! This sort of thing just goes to show that an Atlantic crossing was still something out of the ordinary, and seemingly quite an adventure. He didn't actually get the money before he sailed, for reasons which will become apparent later, but the celebrations must have been a boost to his morale.

This visit lasted a lot longer than the first, almost three months, but there is less information about it despite the fact that his Journals contained an American contribution in almost every issue, under the title "Cribbings from Contemporaries". It would appear that the Journal had a circulation on the other side of the Atlantic, for it is referred to in the "Fall River Advance": "Ben Brierley's Journal is better than ever, and 'Owd Ab' is excelling himself in the production of his vastly interesting sheet." There must have been many Lancashire-dialect-speaking emigrants who could understand the way in which Ab's sketches were written, and whose presence would have made the publication viable.

Ben set sail on the good old City of Berlin on a day that would have done credit to a winter's morning, although it was May: cold and wet. He arrived in the early hours of 12th and went first to Paterson, New Jersey, to renew old acquaintances. Then it was back to New York again, from where he headed for Fall River, Massachusetts, by boat. Here he spent several days as the guest of the Mayor and attended, among other things, a clam-bake. He was impressed by the shops - the early department stores - but also aware of their dangers. "The first I visited was a repository for everything a house requires in the hardware line, from a tin-tack to a bedroom suite. The newly married need not go to any other place for their furnishing, - to Oldham Street for their mahogany; to the Siberia of Knott Mill for their crockery; and to Tom Hudson's for their ironmongery. They can obtain a great deal more than they are perhaps able to pay for without risking a fight with the shower, or being laid under the necessity of chartering a cab."

Whilst in Massachusetts, he was found in the state capital addressing a gathering of the Boston Charitable Society and after a ten-day stay in the area he returned to that little-known spot where the City of Berlin had set him down nearly three weeks earlier - New York.

Whit Monday (2nd June) found him en route for Albany and at the end of the month he was in Great Falls, New Hampshire, where the temperature was a blistering 96 degrees in the shade. The editor of the "Fall River Advance" described Ben's reaction to the heat during a trip out with the paper's religious editor and the driver, Willie Watson. After a short stop, Ben murmured,

"'Say, Watson, drive on a bit. My coat is on fire.' And then, mildly remembering that Brierley really was exposed to the full glare of the sun, and that his everlasting

Nineteenth-century Boston

black cloth suit was absorbing caloric enough to fry eggs in, Willie started the carriage and created a draught.

Drip, drip, drip.

'What is that dripping which I hear?' said our representative to Ben.

'Oh, it's only me, melting,' mournfully replied the suffering poet, 'and I am not sorry it is so if only there is enough of me left to grease a postal card to send home to th'owd rib. I know she'll be glad to have my remains spread upon paper."

The Fourth of July he spent in place called Silver Spring, recuperating from the heat and then on to Newport, Rhode Island, where a dinner was given for him on 11th. Most of the guests were English emigrants and he seems to have felt at home there.

The last week before returning to England was spent in Philadelphia. Here he saw some of the great contrasts of the American dream, writing of a manufacturer who had arrived in America with nothing and risen by his own efforts to become the employer of 3,000 hands and a nominee for a seat in Congress. But he also attended a meeting of a charitable society, the Sons of St George, who raised funds to help the English emigrants who didn't make it; and, just for a change, witnessed one of Buffalo Bill's Wild West shows.

The tour over, he joined the steamer City of Montreal on a cold August morning for the trip back to Liverpool, arriving on Sunday 10th. He wrote "Ab o'th'Yate in Yankeeland", recalling his experiences of both visits and an extract was published in the Manchester Guardian under the title "How Englishmen have Risen in America". It was so well received that a gentleman connected with the American shipping trade asked for a reprint of 50,000 copies!

Before leaving the subject of Ben's foreign travels, let's have a glance at the bound volume of photographs that he took with him on his second trip to America. It languishes in Failsworth Public Library and is not on general display, but may be viewed upon request. Sadly, it is in a very sorry state of repair, at least six of the original photos having been ripped out by a maniac at about the time the book was being moved to the new Robert Sidlow Library from the old Carnegie Library on Oldham Road. Nevertheless, this marvellous piece of local history must have been quite a sight in its younger days: it is a heavy, leather-bound production with metal ornamentation, the entwined letters "B.B." gracing the front cover. Four small metal studs are affixed to the back, acting as table legs. A clasp completes the metalwork and it is whispered that gold was used, but having found no hallmarks on any of the pieces and after tapping the metalwork all over with a magnet, I must conclude that it is gilded brass. The illuminated frontispiece reads, "Presented, with a purse of gold, to Ben Brierley previous to his visiting America... 29th March 1884". John Hall, the Failsworth amateur actor, did the honours and the local scenes (the ones ripped out) were taken by Squire Knott. But the volume also contains portraits of people involved one way or another with Ben's life.

There is a pose of Le Gendre N Starkie, Grand Master of the Masonic Lodges in the Province of East Lancashire, in full regalia, and a host of lesser mortals. A wonderful signed copy of a photograph shows Sam Bamford complete with shoulder-length, snow-white hair and a Father-Christmas beard to match. There's Sam Laycock, striking a pose that would have done credit to a startled shrew. There's Edwin Waugh, appearing severe (although he wasn't), and a prominently placed likeness of Sim Schofield, who looks as

"Furious"

Mad with rage; passion of anger. If yo' want to be put in a proper state have a writ sent yo' for summat someb'dy elze owes, but yo' mun pay. Look o'er th' bankruptcy list, an' find somb'dy "gone" ut owes yo' a lot, an' "assets nil". A two-thri bills thrown in would help th' steeam to get up wonderfully; an' yo'd doance a caper yo' never larnt in a tapreaum. A word or two fro' th' wife, abeaut sarvin someb'dy reet would be as good as a barrowful o' coals on th' fire.

From "Ab o'th'Yate's Dictionary"

though he had just swallowed a goat and left the tail hanging out! I was astonished to find in the collection a full-length shot of Job Ogden, who lived in Bardsley Fold, Failsworth (the site is now covered by the Roman Catholic Church on Lord Lane). Now, "Sober" Job Ogden was Ben's rôle model for Ab o'th'Yate, and in this portrait Job is vertical! The name "Thomas Brierley" on the illuminated frontispiece does not refer to Ben's younger brother Tommy - sadly, he was dead by this time - but to another gifted amateur writer. This Thomas Brierley was a shy and retiring man and the third of five children fathered by an Alkrington hand-loom weaver. His piece "Heaw Quare is this Life" was written in Alkrington on 27th February 1860 and he died in 1909.

The Last Years

1885 was another sad year for Ben. His young friend Tom Nash had not been well and the money from the testimonial fund had still not been handed over. What Ben earned from the American tour wouldn't have lasted long and by the beginning of the year he was under considerable financial strain. Worse was to come. Convinced that he was seriously ill, Nash shot himself in his London office on 28th January, aged only forty. Ben must have been deeply grieved by this news of his benefactor and when on 17th March he was presented with £650 at a dinner laid on for the event, he must have received the testimonial with mixed feelings, to say the least. At the ceremony the delay in handing over the money was blamed only on Mr Nash's removal to London "and other difficulties" - a very Victorian way of dealing with shocking events.

The presentation was made by the Mayor, Alderman Harwood (later Alderman Sir James Harwood. He was born in Oswaldtwistle, near Accrington, in 1832 and came to Manchester in 1853 as a journeyman painter and plasterer), and the money was contained in a purse shaped like a sock! The day after the dinner, the Manchester Guardian reported the event, giving plenty of space to the speech of George Milner, President of the Manchester Literary Club, who praised Ben's writings, comparing him to George Eliot and saying, "Mr Brierley's dialect was as much to be honoured as the dialect in which Burns wrote... It was a dialect which drew its words from the most ancient English sources. It was a dialect which was full of words of great strength and beauty." Good for the Guardian!

The other sad event of the year was the Clifton Hall Colliery disaster. As a result of an explosion on the morning of 18th June, 177 men died and more were injured. Ben was moved to write a poem about it, reproduced in full on page 37 as it shows not only where his loyalties lay, but also that he could write in perfectly good standard English when the mood took him. It gives a vivid picture of the times in which Ben lived and it was printed in the newspaper with notes that make it clear he was thinking of Thomas Worrall, the surviving underlooker of the mine; this man's bravery and that of other colliers who tried to help the injured was praised by the coroner at the inquest. Worrall was knocked unconscious by the blast and when he came to, he saw colliers running for their lives to the pit's eye. Realising that they were likely to be affected by after-damp if they tried to escape in that direction, he told the men to make their way towards Agecroft shaft. "The men at once obeyed him, and begged Worrall to accompany them. This, however, he refused to do, declaring that someone ought to remain as guide to those who, having escaped the fury of the explosion, were yet unable to find their way to the upper ground. The brave fellow at once assumed authority over the panic-stricken workers in the Doe and Five-quarter mine, and undoubtedly, by preventing them from rushing to the Clifton Hall shaft, saved many of them from death by suffocation. He stood at his post until he had reason to believe that every man in the particular mines in which he is underlooker had been sent to the pit's bank."

Le Gendre Starkie in Masonic garb

Worrall was asked to describe the condition of the men underground and the newspaper report of his reply was both detailed and moving: "The fright of the boys and some of the men... was painful to behold. One had become delirious with fear, and began to repeat, in schoolboy fashion, the letters of the alphabet. Men sighed and moaned, some shouted for help, and others muttered words of prayer. All were profusely thankful to find someone to direct them - someone cool and clearheaded enough to calculate the chances of escape and self-denying enough to remain at the post of danger until those under his care were rescued."

Now you've read that, read Ben's poem, "Who are the Brave?" and see what you think. In the midst of his own troubles, he could still feel for others.

Bishop Fraser died in the October, and clearly a great deal of mutual respect had developed between the two men, for the Journal published both a complimentary memorial poem and a letter from the Bishop to Brierley & Firth, dated 1874 and "Never before published". They had written to him, asking permission to publish a portrait and biographical sketch, and his reply was to the effect that he couldn't stop them, but he'd much rather they didn't, together with some complimentary remarks on Ben Brierley's Journal as "healthy literature". They appear to have respected his wishes, and although the memorial poem is unsigned, I wonder whether it was penned by Ben himself, for in praising Bishop Fraser the poet still manages to have a dig at hypocrisy elsewhere in the Church:

What Bishops have been, oft, alas! we see;
He taught us what a Bishop ought to be -
A wise and truthful index to the end,
A loving teacher, and a generous friend.

Despite the testimonial money, the "mansion" in St Oswald's Grove had to go and by 1886 the Brierleys had moved to the less salubrious surroundings of Hall Street, Moston. They weren't reduced to the poverty Ben had known in childhood, for Esther was registered as having shares in the Manchester Ship Canal Company at this address - obviously they were well enough off not to need to cash these in. The house in which Ben died, "The Poplars", no longer stands, but Hall Street does, although it has changed its name to Hillier Street. Early twentieth century author John Ward recalled it being named Ichabod Street on account of its unadopted state. (Ichabod had a most unfortunate start in life. His mother went into labour on learning of the defeat of Israel by the Philistines and the death of her husband in battle, and herself died in childbirth, giving the baby a name which means "the glory is removed from Israel". They knew their Bibles well in the nineteenth century, and everyone would have understood that the nickname was meant to express the forlorn state of the street.)

Let's try to establish exactly where "The Poplars" was. On a Masonic Lodge Summons dated 8th September 1886, Ben's address is given as "The Poplars, Church Lane, Harpurhey". A letter written on 20th October 1889 has it as "The Poplars, Glen Side, Harpurhey" and on letters of 1896 it has become "17 Hall Street, Moston". Of course, all three of these - and other variants I have seen - were the same house. It doesn't help that Moston wasn't incorporated into Manchester until 1890 - about half way through Ben's time there - but the real problem is that the Harpurhey boundary is so close to the site of the house that you could reach out and touch it. Such confusion still exists today. To take a modern example, the house that I used to live in at Chain Bar was officially "Chain Bar, Moston, Failsworth". This was a ploy by the Post Office to suit their own ends - the house never was in Failsworth, it was just that our mail was directed from there. I conclude that Ben's mail was directed from Harpurhey, that's all; and as for Glen Side, the place was pretty rural at the time and it was somebody's attempt to describe where the dwelling was.

Ben's own enforced move lends particular poignancy to his sympathy with the residents of Clock Alley in Manchester, which was about to come down for extensions to the CWS wholesale department. Arthur Shaw, in "The Story of the CWS", sets the scene: "When the site of Balloon Street was a field, Clock Alley lay on its town side, with gardens running into the field. It was the home of fustian cutters and smallware weavers, the latter being makers of 'clock lace' for military facings. By 1885 it had degenerated into a slum, to all appearance dirty and

Who are the Brave?

Who are the brave? They who in battle's strife,
Heedless of danger, charge the unknown foe,
And hand to hand contending - life to life
The stake - the vict'ry won by fatal blow?
Not mine the task to sere the warrior's wreath,
Though red his sword, and blunted in its sheath.

But they are braver who at duty's call,
Far in the reaches of the treacherous mine,
Face dangers that would giant hearts appal,
To save not slay - mercy with love combine -
Firm at their post - no care themselves to save -
The choice 'twixt duty and a threatened grave -

Choose to brave death with blackest terrors drest,
Rather than one should perish by their flight!
And though the blasts of doom might strike the breast,
And sweep them to regions of eternal night,
Heed not repeated calls from Acheron's gate -
"Go, save yourselves, and leave us to our fate."

And this 'mongst shrieks, and prayers, and dying groans,
And jabbering idiotcy, more dreadful still
Than cries for help, or breath-exhausting moans -
The terror-stricken souls with horrors fill;
And showers of wreck rain down upon the way
To blessed hope, the assuring eye of day.

How shall we sing their praise, the noble band,
Who not in knightly joust, or warlike fray,
Rush on each other at a king's command,
But they who Mercy's call at once obey,
Short farewells breathe, then plunge in gloom profound
Uncertain of return to safer ground?

At such brave deeds a nation's heart upheaves,
And pours its blessings with substantial aid;
And hastes to chronicle on virgin leaves
Tributes of praise to none but heroes paid;
And the Great God, in mercy looking down,
Sees in these men the fittest for His crown.

drunken. Nevertheless, the inhabitants included ancient residents of from sixty to ninety-nine years, and sickness was said to be 'scarcely ever heard of'. The demolition of the old double-walled, oak-raftered cottages brought some interesting particulars into the *Manchester City News,* and a contribution by Ben Brierley, the Lancashire author, sent hundreds to visit and revisit the old Alley. In the *Co-operative News* the C.W.S. rent collector explained that actually the cottage interiors had been kept very clean by the dwellers, who made free use of the limewash abundantly supplied. Home is home, and residents in the Alley for fifty years departed only with the greatest reluctance." In the version of his piece which appeared in the Manchester Guardian on 19th September 1885, Ben wrote movingly of one such: "An old fustian cutter who has spent half a century in his garret fairly broke down on his being compelled to leave. All the associations of his life were being separated from him." With his own uprooting imminent, Ben clearly knew how the man felt.

"The Poplars", 17 Hall Street, Moston (from a sketch by A Cantwell)

His straitened financial circumstances didn't prevent Ben fulfilling his public engagements. In 1886 he helped to form the Arthur Sullivan Masonic Lodge (named after the composer Sir Arthur Seymour Sullivan (1842-1900) of Gilbert and Sullivan fame), which met at the Old Boars Head in Withy Grove. The consecration ceremony was performed on 28th June at the Memorial Hall in Albert Square by the Grand Master for East Lancashire, Colonel Le Gendre N Starkie. (Ten years later he signed a dispensation order permitting the wearing of Masonic garb at Ben's funeral.) At the first meeting after the consecration, on 14th July, Ben was invested as Secretary of the Lodge. It must not be thought, however, that Sir Arthur himself was actively involved. He was careful to stipulate, "It is, of course, thoroughly understood that in giving my name to the proposed new Masonic Lodge I am incurring no duties nor responsibilities, and that my personal attendance is not expected," and when he visited Leeds later in the year and Ben sent him a telegram inviting him to visit the Lodge, he politely declined.

The following year Ben was "eating eawt" - pardon me, eating out - again. He was at a gathering at the Queens Hotel in Manchester to celebrate Waugh's attaining his threescore and ten; Ben read his own tribute to his friend.

As pompous treasurer to the Failsworth Local History Society, I feel it only right that I emphasise all Ben's *Failsworth* connections. The foundation stones of Failsworth Liberal Club were laid in 1888 by Lot Hilton of Failsworth and John Fletcher of Ashton-under-Lyne, and the following year Ben gave a speech at the newly-opened club in which he described the area as he had known it fifty years before:-

"No prettier place can be

Sam Laycock, Ben Brierley and friend, photographed by Isaac Wilde of Blackpool, probably in the late 1880s

conceived than was this section of Manchester Road from Watchcote to the canal bridge before the vandals laid their hands upon it and transformed a grand avenue of trees, with its vista beyond lost in the skies, into heaps of bricks and a cricket ground. Our poverty of the past was somewhat compensated by the presence of natural beauty, and our crust was all the sweeter because eaten amidst the quietude of the summer landscape instead of the whirl and the roar of busy life. What sight could have been prettier than the array of white wallets of the handloom weavers as seen on this slope from Watchcote when on their 'bearin'-whom' errands? A quarter of a mile distant you could have heard a footfall. The land on each side of the road was so rich that it grew three crops of grass per year. Now it could only produce brickbats; or, to put the matter in its best light, clusters of cottages, a Town Hall, and a Liberal Club." I bet *that* went down well!

Watchcote - now there's a bone of contention. There *is* a Watchcote Post Office in existence today, but in true Post Office fashion they have sited it in the old Dob Lane. The real Watchcote started higher up, at the Halfway House. But Ben wasn't perfect either. He talks here about the land alongside the road being "so rich", yet elsewhere he wrote, "With a cold soil, imperfectly drained, Failsworth at one time offered but small inducements to husbandry in its more developed sense; so that a century and a half ago the country was little more than an uncultivated waste." Perhaps Failsworth was like the curate's egg, "Exceedingly good in parts."

Ben was back again on October 26th, giving the inaugural speech in celebration of the fact that a third Pole had been erected in Failsworth two months previously. This was one of his last big speeches, so I'll take the liberty of quoting it at length.

"It is a special pleasure to me to be permitted to take part in a celebration in which all parties, whether Conservatives or Radicals in politics, or in religion Churchmen or Dissenters, can join. I was disappointed at not being able to bring the celebrated Eiffel Tower [erected the same year] from Paris to erect it on this spot. - (Laughter.) But I am glad to know that you have got something in its place which, if not quite so stupendous a structure, is, perhaps more suitable for the position it has to occupy. If there be one thing in which I am quite conservative it is in the preservation of our old customs and landmarks, our ancient footpaths, the village greens, the latter of which are being gradually wrested from us. The rushcart died a hard death, not for want of old tub-shaped watches and well-preserved silver spoons that were wont to adorn the sheets. - (Laughter.) But the rushes had ceased to be a necessity in our churches, and the land was being too well-farmed to furnish the rushes. But America can grow timber that can be converted into Maypoles, and the people's loyalty can supply the rest.

We are standing now upon a neutral platform and upon historic ground, for in old times the spirit of township seems to have centred itself about the pole. Possibly a greater number of heads have been broken in fighting political battles where we are now assembled than upon any ground of an equal area in the country, for after the crow came the blow, and feathers would begin to fly at once. In that house (pointing in the direction), next to the one in which I was born, lived old Moffatt, a man reputed to be not only a Jacobin but a Paineite. He was suspected of having in his possession a copy of Paine's 'Rights of Man'. The mob one day gathered about his door and demanded of him the obnoxious book. Old Moffatt retired into his house, and brought out a massive copy of the Holy Bible. 'Gentlemen,' he said, 'this is the only copy of the "Rights of Man"

"Music"

A gift ut's very badly abused. Singin is th' nicest when it's done by someb'dy ut doesno' pretend they con sing. But if they're coed toppers at it, shut yo'r ears, or elze they'n be split. Some folk thinken they con get *music* eaut of a payanna by thumpin it. They dunno' think ut real music should be soft, an' gentle; an' that it should creep into th' soul as if it coome in its stockin feet. A mother doesno' get her babby asleep by yellin a "top note" in its earhole; no more than "Those strains that once did sweet in Zion glide" con be getten eaut of a payanno by tumblin it o'er an' puncin it. When owd Boxer used to play his flute i' th' fowt ov a summer's neet, it seaunded as if some sperrit wur doin it, fields away. That wur music. One yers nowt o'th' sort neaw-a-days. It's o squeal, crash, an' clatter.

From "Ab o'th'Yate's Dictionary"

that I have in my possession.' The mob turned away feeling ashamed of the action they had taken. Happily those things are of the past. They are landmarks such as we do not care to preserve.

The Failsworth of to-day is not the Failsworth of sixty years ago. At the latter period if a meeting of this character had taken place it would have had a different aspect. There would have been no gaily trimmed bonnets, no cloths that were not patched and darned all over, no cheeks that did not betray the presence of pinching poverty. Now behold the contrast. At the coronation of William IV, I assisted in raising the pole which had been taken down to have its vane and points regilded in honour of that event. Child that I was at the time, I can remember how feeble were the voices that joined in singing 'God Save the King'. In contrast to-day will be the voices that will join in singing 'God Save the Queen'. They will come from beneath better padded waistcoats and in more hopeful tones, for since 1830 Failsworth has fixed upon itself the stamp of progress.

The erection of this beautiful emblem of concord is significant of the prosperity you now enjoy. Let us hope that it may be the last, and not have to be, like the Irishman's cabin, taken down for repairs. Its predecessors were raised to commemorate a national event. I hope this youngster may commemorate the extinction of that party rancour which has existed in the township since the days of the Jacobins, when every man trailed his politics as a Donnybrook man trailed his coat for some one to tread upon. The partition which divides parties is now worn so thin that it reminds one of Jack o'Bill's lantern that emitted a better light when there was nothing left but the frame. - (Laughter.) May the fusion of parties give out a more wholesome heat when there is nothing left but the mould. I think the time is not far distant when even that will be demolished and that, as sensible and patriotic Englishmen, we may work together for our common good.

I now declare, in Masonic parlance, that this pole is duly and truly erected, and in the name of the committee and by permission of the Local Board I dedicate it to the people of Failsworth. - (Cheers.)"

Ben, looking old and tired

Ben attended every meeting of the Arthur Sullivan Masonic Lodge. He relinquished his duties as Secretary after two years, but returned to office as Senior Warden on 9th October 1889 and was obviously intended to go forward to the Chair. However, he missed the gathering in March 1890 and although he was there in April and May, there were further absences later in the year. These can be explained by his failing health, as on 18th May he suffered a stroke which left his right side paralysed. He was still struggling to get about in the December and finding it frustrating, for a letter explaining why he could not attend the Manchester Literary Club's Christmas supper refers to his "solitary bear-pit" and complains, "I am chained to my den, where I have to lick my paws alone." The rather spidery signature of his later years was also due to this and the same letter explains that he had only managed to make his writing legible by lashing two fingers together. However, someone had given him a bottle of port to make the struggle more bearable and his sense of humour obviously triumphed as he managed to pen the following lines before closing:

Owd Time - he's a troublesome codger-
Keeps nudgin us on to decay,
An' whispers 'you're nobbut a lodger,
Get ready for gooin away.'

Edwin Waugh had died at the end of April and the same issue of the Manchester Guardian which reported Ben's illness carried a letter suggesting that Waugh's Civil List pension should be transferred to Ben. Attempts were made to get this done, but the Government would only give a grant of £150, saying that this must be regarded as £50 a year for three years. Nonetheless, in the weakened state of Ben's wealth and health it must have been welcome. Less welcome, I should think, was the description of him as "sere and yellow" - which is the epithet given to a leaf as it is about to drop off a tree. A measure of the respect in which he was held was that the Lancashire Members of Parliament united to get Ben this payment from the Royal Bounty Fund.

He was no longer capable of contributing to Ben Brierley's Journal and this folded in 1891. Ben's farewell to his readers was both dignified and touching: "The unpleasant duty has devolved upon me of announcing that with the present number the publication of *Ben Brierley's Journal* will be discontinued. For years I have been unable, through physical infirmities, to perform the mechanical work required of an editor. Under these circumstances the proprietors of the journal, Messrs ABEL HEYWOOD & SON, have generously offered to relieve me of further anxiety by withdrawing it from publication. It is something to say that for a period of over twenty years there has scarcely been a number issued without my hand being seen in it. This means a great deal of work, which has at times been irksome. But 'the labour we delight in physics pain'. I now seek the bodily rest which for sixty years I have not known, only such as has been necessitated by sickness, which is only cessation from work. Perhaps it would not be too much to ask of the public this little indulgence for the short time I have to live. Goodbye! BEN BRIERLEY."

The following year a fund was set up to provide him with an income and a meeting was called to think of the best way to provide funds: "Typically it was at a meeting called by the Liberal Lord Mayor of Manchester, and supported by the Mayors of several other towns, that the Appeal Committee was formed, with an active Tory councillor in the city as secretary, and although the subscriptions ranged from a shilling upwards, the letters and publicity spotlight the prominent contributors - Lord Derby, at least six Tory and Liberal MPs, and a string of big industrialists." Ben had been a Freemason for seventeen years by this time, and, quite rightly, they helped their brother all they could.

"Siesta"

A short sleep in the afternoon. When yo' con get it. If there's a youngster abeaut, or a blue-bottle flee, yo'n no' get forty winks at one howd. I hardly know which is th' biggest plague o' th' two. One goes buzz, buzz, reaund yo'r yead; an' if there's no thatch on, it'll have a bit of a ramble o'er th' top. If a youngster's i' th' place, it'll oather climb yo'r knees, or th' cheear back.

From "Ab o'th'Yate's Dictionary"

Ben found the publicity given to the fund raising humiliating, as had his old friend Sam Bamford before him. Anyone who thinks state pensions should be abolished ought to read Ben's letter which appeared in the Manchester Guardian of 4th March, and think about how he must have felt. It says much for the character of the man that he was able to write about his own situation so courageously and honestly.

"Sir - The meeting on Tuesday last has placed me in a very awkward position. I am bound to *admit* that I am poor without being *actually* so. Had the gentlemen who spoke said I was getting old and too infirm to do much more work they would have been about right. They might know what it would lead to in the ordinary course of things. But I have no fear of immediate poverty; and I have a soul above showing my hat lining until necessity forces me. It will be a year or two before the 'wolf' scratches the paint off my front door. I have not lived an extravagant life. Brought up a working man, I have since lived as a working man. That enables me to say I owe no man a penny. I wish everybody could say the same. I should be a richer man if they could. When this matter was first named to me I expressed a wish that I could meet my friends socially, and not be stopped in the public street to receive their congratulations, because that involves much physical pain. I mentioned a concert at the Free-trade Hall. That would not compromise my feeling of independence, nor give me the appearance of a beggar. I commend this suggestion to the gentlemen who have formed the committee. I write at great personal inconvenience to set myself right with the public. - I am, &c., BEN BRIERLEY Moston, March 3, 1892."

It didn't do him any good financially - in fact the Secretary of the fund-raising committee commented rather testily that they'd have made twice as much money if he hadn't written it. But it preserved his self-respect. And he did get £356, which was presented to him in the October.

This glowing tribute from the "History and Annals of Blackley", published in 1892, is another indication of how highly Ben was regarded by his contemporaries. It was written by Peter Ball, under his pseudonym of "Philip Wentworth". "I regret very much that I have not been able to find room for a specimen of Ben Brierley's prose composition. My hope is that the readers of this history will have complete copies of his works which ought to be in the private libraries of all who live in Lancashire, and can afford to buy them. The day is coming when they will become greatly enhanced in value, not only because of their scarcity, but because they will be better understood. True it is that the Lancashire dialect has a little gone out of fashion, probably because those who wrote in it were mere catch-penny scribes, whose humour was constrained and unnatural, and whose wit was laborious and spasmodic. But good writing even in the dialect, can never be wholly out of fashion, although it may languish for want of extensive patronage; but as sure as the sun that sets in the west to-night will rise again in the east to-morrow so surely will the dialect come in fashion again. But whether it does or not the works of Brierley are immortal because they are works of genius. And this praise he specially deserves. He addressed himself to the toiling millions of Lancashire wage-earners, described the characters that were best known to them, gave utterance to their joys and sorrows, and to their aspirations and struggles. It has been too much the fashion among local critics and connoisseurs of late years to compare and contrast Brierley with Waugh for the purpose of disparagement. Criticisms founded on contrast and comparisons of this kind are absolutely worthless. The fact is Waugh had an originality, a method, and domain of his own, and Brierley owes no man anything. He is master in his own house, and well he has conducted and furnished it. I fear to say more lest the truth should be mistaken for flattery."

Ben Brierley (left). The other two gentlemen are believed to be Richard Rome Bealey (seated) and John Cropper, MA, the Unitarian parson at Stand when Ben stayed there

Sim Schofield, too, paid tribute to his lasting concern with the welfare of others, and to his independent spirit. When Ben was "in a weak state of health and could scarcely walk", Sim took a carriage to his house to take him to the polling booth. "'Nay, nay, Sim,'" said Ben, "'aw'm noan gooin' t'begin a-ridin' neaw. Aw shall walk to th'poll.' He took my arm, and walk he did. I only wish we had more Ben Brierleys in this respect." He kept his sense of humour as well. The response when Sim told him of a "keen political fight" in Failsworth, in which one of Ben's old friends had stood as Tory candidate, was "'What, an' has owd So-an'-So turned Tory? Well, that caps o'. Why, his feythur were at Peterloo in 1819 with thine an' mine, Sim. But then,' remarked Brierley, after reflecting a little, 'aw'd forgettun he's begun a keepin' an alehouse, an' he's gettin' too well off to be a Radical.'"

Life was hard for him physically, but he kept his intelligence and his gift for language. At the presentation of his testimonial in 1892, he referred to his enforced solitude after his stroke two and a half years earlier. It is one of the best descriptions of an old man sitting and thinking alone that I have ever read: - "In those solitary hours he had so often reviewed his life, and so often lived it over again, that he had come to regard it as a life that he had lived when some other being. Scenes and events occurred to his memory in forms that resembled the pieces of coloured glass in a kaleidoscope - fantastic imagery that he could not separate from the real. Were the characters he had attempted to describe in his books people he had met, or were they creations of the brain? He was sometimes puzzled to distinguish... He had lived among his creations. They had been his companions when other society had been denied him." And he was rightly proud of them. "He had aimed to make men and women better and happier by those creations. If he had succeeded, well and good. If he had failed, it was in a righteous cause." Not many of us have as clear a conscience as that!

His name is missing from the street directories after 1891 - probably he wasn't well enough to cope with visits or correspondence from strangers - but he and Esther continued to live at Hall Street and it was there that he died, at midnight on Saturday, 18th January 1896. On the following Monday Charles G Skinner certified the cause of death as disease of the heart/dropsy and Ben's nephew, Harold Berry, was present (he was a cashier living at 25 Petworth Street, Cheetham, although the death certificate spells it "Pepworth"). It was the custom to give mourners sprigs of rosemary (for remembrance) to be worn as a buttonhole, and to be dropped into the grave after the coffin had been lowered. In his 1920s book, "The Old Road", James Middleton recalls, "The last time I saw rosemary at a funeral was at the burial of Ben Brierley when Charles Potter, the artist, advanced across the bedroom and laid the sprig of rosemary on the breast of his dead friend as a last tribute of affection."

The following lines are probably the last which Ben wrote, and they reveal a more serious side of his character which was known only to his most intimate friends. Esther found them a few days after his death, written in lead pencil, among the papers he had last handled.

Song of the Angels

Round the great Creator's throne,
Hear the loud hosannas ring.
Earth is silent when 'tis known
We can hear the angels sing.

How sweetly now the music steals
Through the air in liquid strains;
Each tone the sacred truth reveals,
That in Heaven Jehovah reigns.

Ben was buried on Wednesday 22nd January in Harpurhey General Cemetery, next to his beloved daughter Annie. Non-family mourners included members of the Manchester Literary Club, representatives from several Masonic lodges and a wide range of friends and admirers. For some obscure reason Mr W Goldthorpe, Chairman of Salford Hundred Quarter Sessions, put in an appearance, as did Charles Potter, James and John Dronsfield, James Middleton, Samuel Gradwell, Robert Dottie and Sim Schofield - who must have suffered from foresight because, according to his memoirs, he turned up a year early! It was Sim who wrote the verse attached to the wreath sent by the poor weavers of Failsworth:

This picture of Ben is said to have been taken about 1882. However, the drawn face and slightly unkempt hair suggest that a more likely date is 1892

The weavers of Failsworth this floral harp send,
A tribute of love to their author and friend.

Memorials and Other Matters

Two sides of the Brierleys' square, tapering memorial are blank. A third bears the verse to Annie already mentioned and the words "In loving memory of Annie, only child of Ben and Esther Brierley of Collyhurst, who died June 13th 1875, aged 18 years & 7 months." The last side reads, "In loving memory of Ben Brierley, who died Jan 18th 1896, in his 71st year. Also Esther, beloved wife of the above Ben Brierley, who died on her 80th birthday, May 25th 1914." The stone was restored in 1936 at the expense of Fred Day of Failsworth.

To locate Ben's grave, stand at the open gates of the cemetery on Rochdale Road and walk 120 paces down the drive. On your left a tall, square stone dedicated to the memory of John Alger can easily be seen. Turn 90 degrees left and walk (or push) your way about 40 paces towards the wall of the adjacent Queens Park. You should now be on, or by, the spot.

The park adjacent to the cemetery opened for business on 22nd August 1846 "One was a park for the living, and one a park for the dead", as someone subtly put it! Two years after Ben's death a magnificent Portland stone statue of him was erected in the park. It must have been quite a spectacle at the unveiling when the stone was pure white and the one-and-a-third life-size statue was revealed standing on its massive plinth facing the museum. The stone came from Dorset, the sculptor was John Cassidy and the words on the plinth read:

"Ben Brierley 1825-1896
In prose and verse and in
the dialect spoken by themselves
He set forth with great
faithfulness and power
the life of the working-folk
of Lancashire.
Erected by public subscription
April 1898.

In my early days there were few schools to help us in the pursuit of learning. If we wanted to climb we had first to make our own ladders."

According to "A Walk Round Manchester Statues" by Derek Brumhead and Terry Wyke (1990), it was "the city's first statue to a literary figure and a working-class man".

The years have not been kind to Ben's statue. The Manchester weather, combined with soot and what we now call acid rain, did not enhance the soft, white stone, causing the features to weather away and leaving him with a blank expression and an apparent shortage of waistcoat buttons! The lower left arm and the sheets of lead (representing paper) which he held in his left hand were already missing in 1977, when the Ben Brierley celebrations were held in Queens Park. The plinth has fared better, being made of harder stone, and can still be seen in one piece (a figurative expression - close examination reveals that it is made up of at least eleven pieces almost imperceptibly married). Having survived two World Wars, the statue finally met its doom between a quarter to ten and a quarter past eleven one night in late July or early August 1980 - "Pulled down by the use of ropes". The broken pieces were salvaged and laid silently near the Lodge on Rochdale Road until they were taken to the old Lakeside Café in Heaton Park. The authors of "A Walk Round Manchester Statues" say, "At the present time there appears little hope that 'Owd Ben'... will return to his pedestal." I have to agree with them, having seen the state he is in, with bits and pieces missing and the lead gone - for a weigh-in, no doubt. But if *I* win the pools, he will!

Never mind, John Cassidy's plaster bust "mock up" for the head can still be viewed. Now it stands on a wooden pedestal, bearing a plaque which reminds us that it was donated by Sim Schofield, in a corner of the Failsworth Library. Previous locations were halfway up the stairs in the Failsworth Liberal Club; in the council chambers on Oldham Road (at least there is a photograph, circa 1949), and at one point in Sim's front room at Auburn Bank, New Moston. The bust too has suffered from the attention of vandals - chewing gum in the eyes, rude remarks on the forehead and so on - but it survives, as a reminder of Ben and of the sculptor John Cassidy (1860-1939). Cassidy was born in Ireland and studied at the Manchester School of Art. He first started as a sculptor in 1887 and modelled over two hundred heads for Queen Victoria's Jubilee Exhibition. As well as Ben's statue, he modelled (among others) Sir Benjamin Dobson for Bolton and some for the John Rylands Library in Manchester.

I don't know whether he also did the tablet which marks Ben's birthplace, but this was paid for with surplus funds after the statue was put up. A contemporary newspaper report describes a visit by ten members of the committee, including George Milner, John Dronsfield, W E Clegg, John Cassidy and the ubiquitous Sim Schofield. "On arriving at Failsworth the party were photographed by Mr W Diggle, of Oldham, and afterwards adjourned to the Crown and Cushion Inn ["Th'Owd Bell" of Ben's "Ab o'th'Yate" sketches], where a pleasant time was spent. Mr Milner proposed the toast 'May the tablet remain for generations undisfigured and untarnished, and

Queen's Park, in the days when Ben still watched over it

may the same wish be fulfilled with regard to the fame of Ben Brierley.' Leaving Failsworth the party drove to Queen's Park to view the statue." I'm sure Ben would have approved of this 'pleasant time' spent in his memory!

Try as I may, I can't track down the portrait of Ben painted by George Perkins about 1890. Perkins was born about 1840 and studied at the Manchester School of Art, specialising in landscapes and portraits. He exhibited in Manchester between 1877 and 1896 and in 1890 was President of the Athenaeum Club. He is known to have exhibited a portrait of Ben - presumably a drawing - that year and was living at Glenfield Terrace, Clough Side, Blackley, though by 1893 he had moved to Apsley Place, 131 Rochdale Road, Harpurhey. He died comparatively young in 1897.

Sim Schofield went to see the finished portrait with Ben, and I'll quote his account in the hope that he got it right this time! "On leaving the artist's studio Brierley said, 'Sim, I should feel honoured if that picture could be placed in some institution in Failsworth, so that my old friends and neighbours could look at it when I am gone.'" Sim promised to see that this was done and "In a few days we raised sufficient funds (twenty-five guineas) among the working folk of Failsworth to purchase the picture, and to-day [1905] it hangs on the walls of the Failsworth Liberal Club. The price of the picture was fifty guineas, but the artist promised me, if it could be hung in Failsworth, we could have it at half-price."

Ben Brierley, from the painting by George Perkins which once hung in Failsworth Liberal Club

The painting certainly hung there for some years alongside a portrait of the Failsworth actor John Hall, and it was photographed in the council building, along with the bust. A report in a Manchester paper in - I think - the 1950s claimed that the painting had been rescued from a tip by somebody who recognised it for what it was - or perhaps they fancied the frame! If you know where it is, please inform me - *I'll* give you a fiver for it. It must have given Ben great satisfaction to be so honoured by the Athenaeum's President, for it was the Athenaeum which had so savagely reviewed some of his earlier work. "They cut me up dreadfully," said Ben, referring to this early criticism, "but they gradually began to see me in a better light."

Looking at Ben in a Masonic light, his name lives on in the Ben Brierley Lodge, the Ben Brierley Chapter and the Ben Brierley Lodge of Instruction. Who would have thought that the ragged, semi-starved lad plying the bobbin wheel and hand-loom would rise to become one of the best-loved provincial writers of his time and after his death would have no fewer than three Masonic institutions named after him?

It is a curious experience to read a modern bus timetable and have the name "Ben Brierley" catch your eye, but it can be done - some of Greater Manchester's vehicles even bear the name on their destination plates, as the terminus is outside the Ben Brierley Hotel at the junction of Moston Lane and Kenyon Lane - another lasting memorial to Ben. Whilst I was "on research" in the tap room some years ago, the barmaid informed me that the cellar was haunted, but I felt it my duty to point out to her that it wasn't the ghost of Ben himself

The plaster bust in Failsworth Library which was the model for John Cassidy's statue

floating around the barrels, as he died in 1896 and the pub, formerly an Openshaw Brewery house, wasn't built until 1899, so he never knew of its existence. On the other hand, it *is* built on the site of the former "Long Vault", which was two old cottages knocked into one. Whoever painted the swinging sign that creaks on the Moston Lane side of the pub should be locked up. The artist can never have seen a likeness of our hero and has him looking like a semi-demented caveman, grasping a quill. I'm sure Ben did use a quill in his time, but even I have an "Empire" typewriter of 1892 and I should think he tapped a key or two in his later years, especially after the stroke which affected his right side and made it difficult to control a pen. It's not too hard to tap out a manuscript with one finger, as this book will testify. Whilst I was in the "Ben", sipping a fruit juice and waiting for the rain to stop, I produced a photograph of Ben Brierley and passed it round the room for comments by the regulars, in case they had a scrap of information on him which might have come in useful: "Ooze that, Abrum Lincun?" Well, now they know!

Acknowledgements

Thanks are due to the following people and organisations for their help with information and illustrations for this book:

G Brierley of Lytham St Anne's; John Butterwick, for information from his vast private library; Bury Library; A Cantwell of Moston for the drawing of "The Poplars"; Chetham's Library; Mr Clare Dunkerley of Hale (born Failsworth); Ross Eckersley, for information on the Reverend John Cropper; Failsworth Libary; Peter Fox, Oldham Museum; Morris Garratt; Frank Heaton, for the photograph of Wood Street Mission children; Ian Jones, Manchester Unity of Oddfellows, for his courtesy and for permission to reproduce items from the Oddfellows Magazine; Manchester Central Library - Archives, Language and Literature, Local Studies, Microfilm Unit and Social Sciences Departments; Sandra Martin, Manchester City Art Galleries; Radcliffe Library; Salford Local History Library; Arthur Shaw of Failsworth, for "bringing up" old photographs; Swinton Library, for information on the Clifton Hall Colliery disaster; Chris Watkins, Rochdale Local Studies Library; and all whose ears I have bent while on research for Ben Brierley's biography.

Special thanks are due to Edwin Banks for proof-reading the manuscript, and for correcting my schoolboy howlers.

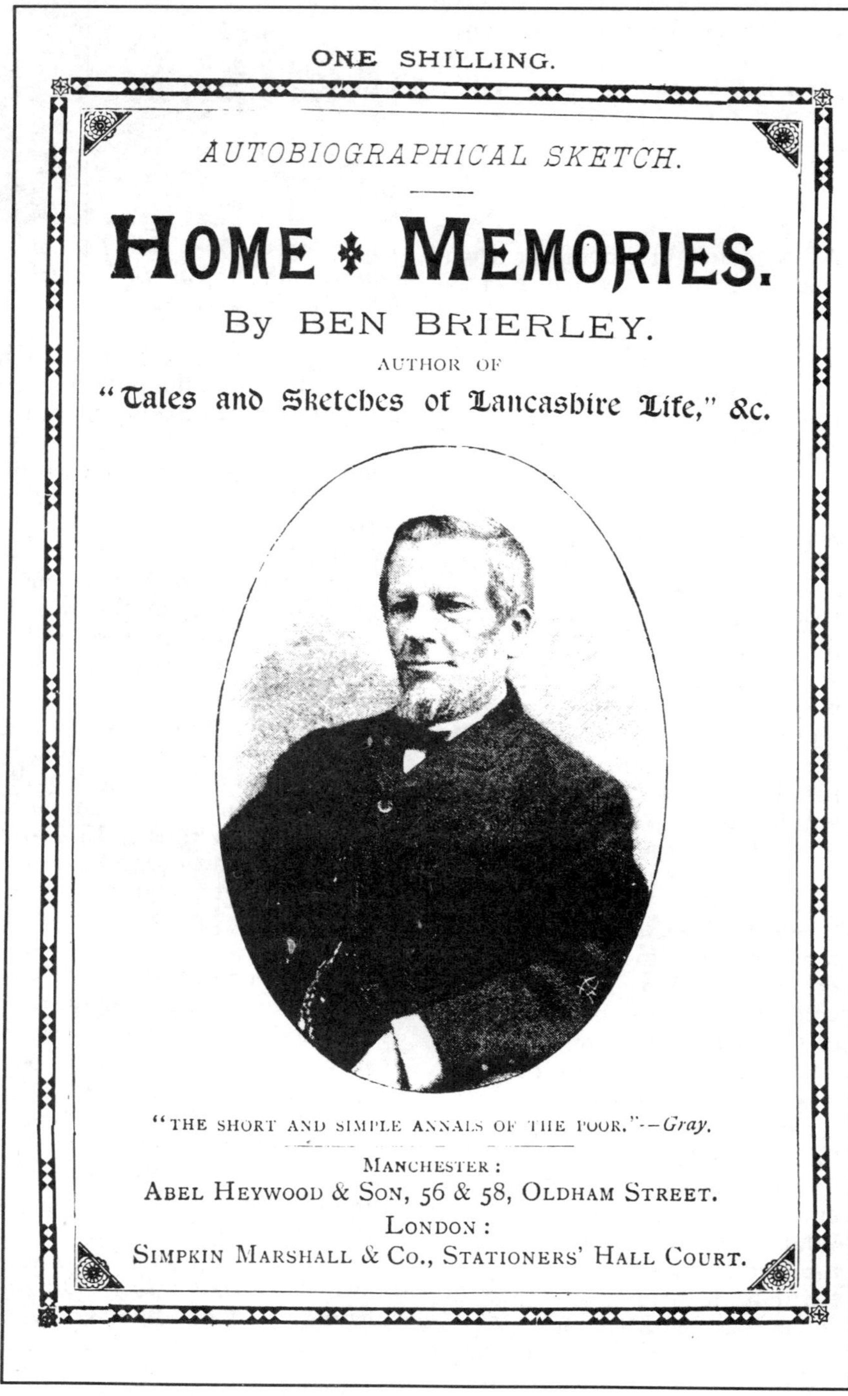

ONE SHILLING.

AUTOBIOGRAPHICAL SKETCH.

HOME MEMORIES.

By BEN BRIERLEY.

AUTHOR OF

"Tales and Sketches of Lancashire Life," &c.

"THE SHORT AND SIMPLE ANNALS OF THE POOR."—*Gray.*

MANCHESTER:
ABEL HEYWOOD & SON, 56 & 58, OLDHAM STREET.
LONDON:
SIMPKIN MARSHALL & CO., STATIONERS' HALL COURT.

Short Bibliography

Ben Brierley's Journals, 1869-1891

Various editions of Ben Brierley's works and memoirs

Various editions of Manchester street directories and newspapers

Various periodicals such as those of the Manchester Literary Club and the Oddfellows Magazine

William Axon, The Annals of Manchester (1886)

William Axon, An Architectural and General Description of the Town Hall (1878)

Dennis Ball, The Story of Failsworth (1973)

Edwin Banks, The Story of Ben Brierley and his Contemporaries (1979)

Samuel Bamford, Diary (1858-1861), held by Manchester Archives

Jean and Peter Bond, Tim Bobbin Lives (1986)

Robert Dottie, The Rambles and Recollections of 'R Dick' (1898)

James Dronsfield, Ouselwood (reprinted 1921)

Clare Dunkerley, 'Ben Brierley (Ab o'th'Yate) 1825-1896' in Transactions of the Manchester Association for Masonic Research LXVII (1977)

Nigel Dyckhoff, The Cheshire Lines Committee (1984)

Failsworth Industrial Society Jubilee History (1909)

J K Hardman, 'List of Fines' from Britain 1760-1870 (1975)

Charles Hardwick, Pilgrimage through Collyhurst (1883)

Sheila H Lazarus, Life and Times of Ben Brierley (1964) (Unpublished thesis held by Manchester Central Library's Archives Department)

Gary S Messinger, Manchester in the Victorian Age (1985)

James Middleton, The Old Road (1920)

Freda Millett, Childhood in Oldham, 1890-1920 (1989)

Sim Schofield, Short Stories About Failsworth Folk (1905)

William Trevor, Playtimes in a Busy Life (1909)

P Wentworth, History and Annals of Blackley (1892)